The Quantum Vocalist

The Singer's Formula to Vocal Balance and Bliss

By Faith Powers

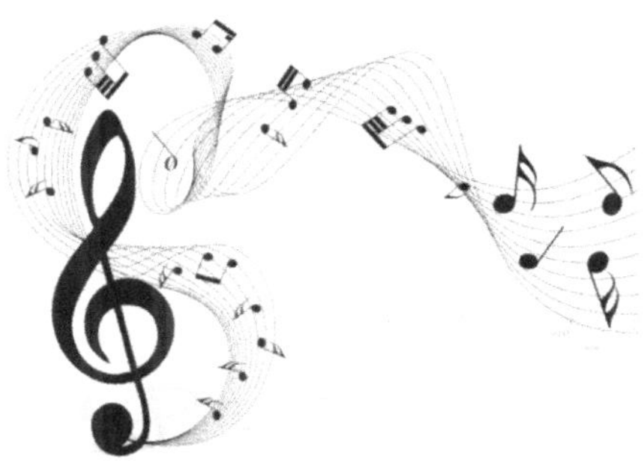

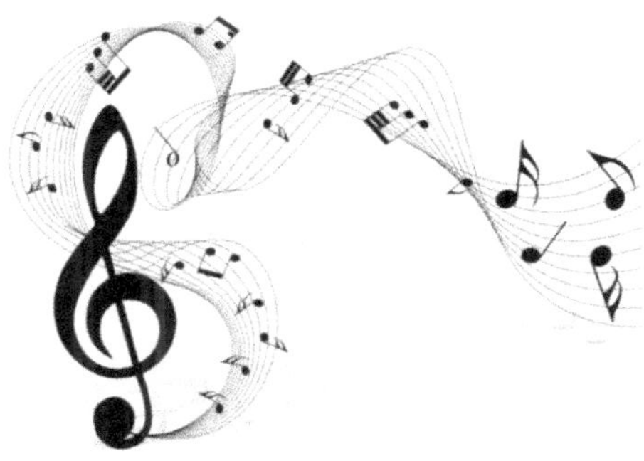

Dedication

I dedicate this book to the remarkable fact that our voices actually hold the key to global harmony. This literary work of art is written in the deepest gratitude to my extraordinary spiritual guides, including my blessed husband, whom I had the good fortune to meet along the way. They have revealed a much deeper understanding of expression and connection to the intuitive spiritual voice. It is also dedicated to God's many Angels & Avatars and to the memory of my spiritual teachers, who have profoundly illuminated my world. Most of all, it is dedicated to our most blessed Lord for giving me the most wonderful life through devotional arts and music, a life that has been an amazing, magical, and blessed journey.

A deeply spiritual friend once said, "Life is about an opportunity to purify, to become hallowed so we can fly high as we cultivate a blissful epic inner world. I believe we are all winners, all the time, when we embrace our higher calling. God knows why He created us; therefore, trust in Him, and something good will come out of every situation. We all have a divine purpose. Just like a brush stroke on His divine canvas, we are an intrinsic part of this majestic Godly art and plan. In this way, our voices hold the key to God's global harmony.

We live in two realities that exist side by side. The choice is up to us to dwell in the higher realms whenever and wherever possible.

I further dedicate this book to all those who love to sing, especially those who embrace devotional, inspiring, positive, or spiritual songs;

May your voice bring happiness, inner peace, and comfort to you and those around you.

I send my well wishes to my students worldwide. May you all continue to illuminate, save, and transform the world into a better place with the power and grace of your voices raised in divine song.

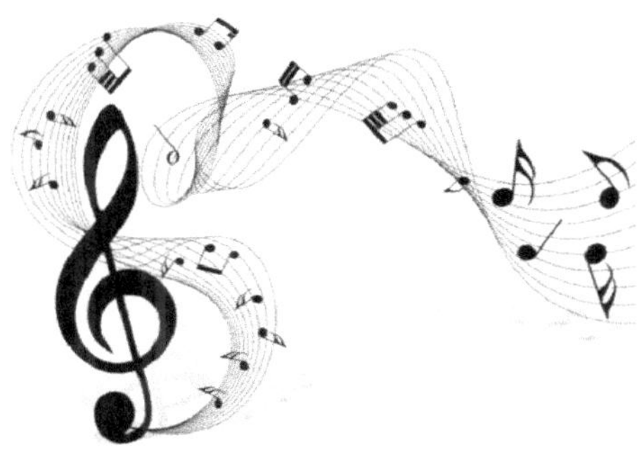

Contents

CHAPTER TWO: Your Vocal Anatomy

CHAPTER THREE: Vocal Mapping

CHAPTER FOUR: The Vocal Embouchure

CHAPTER NINE: Nurturing Your Voice

CHAPTER TEN: A Higher Calling

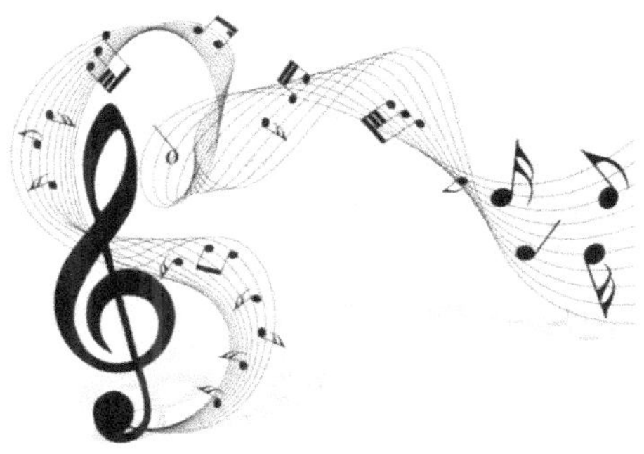

Foreword

This book is designed to support you in your inspired singer's journey. I am presenting the tools needed to take your singing to the next level, which is as unlimited as your imagination and as vast as your wildest dreams. With a divinely bestowed creative passion, artistic focus, and resolute inner determination, anything is possible.

This book is designed to bring solace, empowerment, purpose, transformation, enlightenment, and hope to all those who love to sing. If you are a novice vocalist, let me take the mystery out of singing and help you discover the magical voice you dream about. For professional singers, I offer gems of wisdom to empower you so you can sing effortlessly at higher levels of performance.

I started singing at age five when my mother, a coloratura soprano and master of the three voices, encouraged me. She would tell me that my voice could bring tears of happiness to the angels. The gifts of singing and dancing have been with me during my entire life, sanctioned by both my material and spiritual families. Most of all, they were sanctioned by the Supreme Lord, who is the abode from which the embodiment of all artistic goodness flows.

My voice, when infused with divine intention, has brought me innumerable hours of bliss, inner comfort, contentment, artistic satisfaction, and happiness through singing and the power of the spoken word. It is my goal to gift this treasure trove of happiness to all of you.

These wonderful vocal modalities, when infused with devotional vibrations, will have a profound impact on your listeners. It will offer them immense peace and profound inner transformation of body, mind, and soul in the most magical and miraculous ways. This book will help you share your inner riches with everyone, so that you can have a vibrant inner life that brings radiant happiness and peace to your everyday existence. When you practice the sublime vocal programs presented here, you can leverage your voice's natural beauty and ability. This will bring about a positive shift in your life, allowing you to experience happiness and heaven now.

My husband wisely says, "One just needs to become a good human being."

Many great teachers encourage us to treat others with kindness and compassion, to be grateful and content. They ask us to love fully and unconditionally, and to have a well-polished compass. Above all, let's love God with our hearts and souls, which will protect us on all levels. These basic principles are a magic formula, the God code, and the heavenly pathway to perpetual peace. I believe we can sing our way to a brighter day. It's never too late to be spiritually great! As Winston Churchill said, "Never, never give up!"

Your voice is a brilliant gift from the Creator. When you use it with fervor, warmth, and emotional buoyancy in interpersonal communications, in prayer, in devotional singing, in chanting, in spoken affirmations or in modalities like hypnotherapy or NLP (neuro-linguistic programming), it can have life-changing and life-saving results.

Once, when I was in tremendous pain in the hospital emergency room, an angelic voice told me to listen to a hypnotherapy NLP recording that I had on my iPhone. Being certified in Hypnotherapy and NLP, I had created the recording for myself. "I might as well give it a try," I thought.

Within a few minutes, the pain suddenly, magically, miraculously, completely disappeared. I remember strolling happily out of the emergency room although the doctors were insisting that I needed emergency surgery.

Cultivating your voice and its many wonderful attributes is your God-given right, and it can save your life! Your voice is God's everlasting gift to you and your gift to Him. With that in mind, go forth with a heart brimming with gratitude and cultivate it into a brilliant gift to God. This holy intention set into motion will assist you in achieving the best possible life. Knowing how to use your voice can help you get through the most challenging times.

Your songs give a voice to your heart, allowing access to your innermost sanctum of emotions, dreams, and frailties, revealing the core of your unique essence. The voice can bring solace, empowerment, purpose, and hope to anyone who loves to sing or talk, uncovering the magical power and beauty within each individual sound signature. Your voice allows you to create a dramatic shift within, so you can influence the world around you in the most miraculous ways. You can console the inconsolable and make those who feel unlovable, feel loved. The loving, positive, caring, kind, and compassionate words you speak or sing, infused with sincere intonations and balanced resonance, can bring a wilting heart back to life and give faith to those who need it the most. You can transform the world around you into a much more inspiring, loving, and kinder place.

This book will provide you with everything you need to access your own angelic voice and use it to the fullest. Along this journey, I will offer you a variety of tools to support you as a vocalist, and in the process, to help you discover your vocal balance and the personal bliss of transformational enlightened singing. I have included a comprehensive explanation of how your voice works. I have also provided practical, hands-on guidance that will help strengthen and rejuvenate your voice as well as giving you a dynamic connection among the three voices: chest, middle, and head. In this way, you can care for your entire being which is your most cherished instrument. I have included body, mind, and spirit wisdom from some of the top health experts in the world. As a bonus, **I am offering the Quantum Vocalist diet, a gift to me from the angels, which helped cure me from lupus.**

Finally, I will help you discover and develop the naturally authentic voice that resides within you, your very own heavenly instrument. This book was written with you in mind. Whether you think you can sing or not, I am confident that you will be able to use your voice as a beautiful and compelling window into the artistic nature of your soul.

Starting from the core of your heart, I will guide you on a wonderful sublime voyage, a voyage that will help you break through all the boundaries of the self. This journey will help you release your own unique song from the depths of your heart. I always say, "Sing your prayers and dance your dreams because life is sacred art in motion and your most treasured gift to God."

Singing is so potent, it can help change the way your brain functions. When you're depressed, anxious, or irritated, singing positive, inspired spiritual songs can instantaneously uplift your mood and free you from negative thoughts and emotions. Theoretically, the singing process can give you access to over twenty thousand dollars' worth of feel-good chemicals that naturally reside within your brain. A part of the singing process includes breath work that helps stimulate these chemicals, calming your body and shifting your mental state.

A scientific study done in 2015 at the Eric Whitacre Singers concert demonstrated that both listening to music and singing reduce stress. The study, led by scientists at the Centre of Performance Science at the Royal College of Music and Imperial, included fifteen singers and forty-nine audience members ranging from seasoned concert-goers and musicians to classical music novices who were hooked up to ECG monitors. After submitting saliva samples and completing a questionnaire, singers and audience members experienced decreases in their levels of stress hormones. The Royal College of Music team collected extraordinary data while working with Tenovus Choirs, seeing measurable benefits from singing among cancer patients.

The bottom line is that singing positive, inspiring, and devotional music is good for you and for those around you. Are you convinced yet? Are you ready to get started? Turn the page and let's get going so you can have the voice you've always dreamed of.

—*Faith Powers*

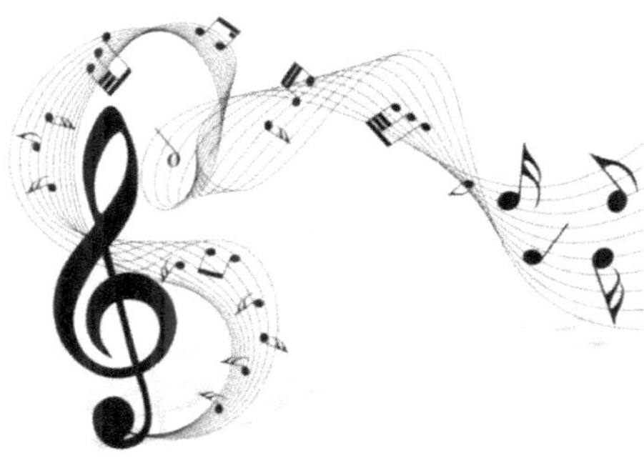

Introduction

The Quantum Vocalist Method

The Quantum Vocalist (QV) is a revolutionary vocal training method that maximizes and leverages your own naturally beautiful vocal abilities. This method can be applied to any style of singing. It will offer you a greater expanded vocal presence and influence your singing voice. The technique is an accumulation of the world's finest vocal methods, currently being used by hundreds of Grammy winning vocalists, *New York Times* best-selling authors, World Class speakers and presenters, as well as Academy Award winning actors, Metropolitan Opera singers, and Broadway stars.

Celebrated singers, speakers, actors, and actresses have used the QV method as a way to perfect their vocal presences and empower their speech. In many cases, the QV method can help rehabilitate a performer's voice that has sustained damage caused by substandard vocal methods or years of incorrect vocal techniques and application habits. QV training will improve your singing while allowing you to sing with greater vocal health and greater vocal range for a more robust on-stage presence. It can resolve gaps and/or shifts in the tone and resonance quality throughout your entire range. Simply by utilizing the QV method, you will avoid a loss of vocal strength in areas that are prone to shifts such as the middle or upper vocal ranges. And you will be able to maintain a solid and powerful connection even while traversing the three voices (chest, middle, and head). Finally, the Quantum Vocalist will help you discover a greater vocal freedom, inspired creative expression, and impressive power, all enveloped with rich resonance and vibrant clarity.

What the Quantum Vocalist Method Can Do for You

The Quantum Vocalist method will uncover your natural, beautiful instrument by giving you expert world-class guidance in the vocal process. You will learn to maximize your anointed instrument and uncover your brilliantly beautiful voice.

Rule of thumb: "IF YOU CAN SPEAK, YOU CAN SING"

One day with masterful guidance can take your voice to the next level. It is possible to become a musical muse, an angelic songbird at any age using Quantum Vocalist, an innovative vocal method that applies cutting-edge, scientifically proven Quantum tools to help guide you on your vocal journey. It blends the best of the best, and creates an amalgamation of the physics of singing with the intangible, intuitive, spiritual art of vocal expression. This fusion creates a voice that is both sublime and divine.

In order to become a good singer, you will need to develop a dedication to regular practice and attentive repetition. This daily practice regime is a subtle form of brain reprogramming. When you wrap your consciousness around a daily or weekly practice, you will attract and manifest these thoughts or moods in your life experience. This repetition can effortlessly train and tame your brain in such a pleasurable and powerful manner. It will transform your life in the most amazing and miraculous ways.

In the May 2, 2003, issue of the *Journal of Personality and Social Psychology*, a study revealed a direct link between singing and listening to negative songs with violent concepts in schools, communities, and places of worship. For this reason, I encourage singers and performers to choose healthy, uplifting, positive spiritual music. If you are engaged in making positive sonic sounds, you will experience vibrant health and happiness, which are healing to the body, mind, and soul.

With the QV method, you will learn about optimum health and the care of your voice through the latest in holistic and anti-aging medicine, including eating super foods. You are the divine instrument so the better you take care of your body, the more exceptional your singing will be and the greater global change agent you will become. The by-product magic of this process is that you will most likely be more loved, adored, and respected by all.

The Creation of QV

With more than twenty years of experience, dedication, and rigorous training in the performing arts and vocal coaching arenas, I bring you my years of research and intuitive development. I have trained with some of the finest vocal coaches in the world and at the most prestigious music institutes. My method combines instinctive sensibilities with scientific formulas and practical applications to create remarkable and award-winning results. This highly effective vocal training technique can now be used to help any vocalist, actor, or speaker accelerate rapidly in order to swiftly reach their full vocal potential.

The development of the "sympathetic, intuitive ear," helps diagnose a vocalist's problems with methodical precision, and often within a matter of minutes.

Positive response from distinguished clients and their families has ignited my fervor to reach out and teach this distinctive, formulated vocal method to vocalists worldwide. Over the years, I have worked with Grammy winners, *American Idol* and *The Voice* vocalists, Emmy winners, Academy Award winners, Broadway leads, Metropolitan Opera vocalists, *Destination Stardom* winners, *New York Times* best-selling authors, and *Fortune 500* industry leaders to help perfect their vocal presence and power.

At the Quantum Vocalist, we are known for our extensive knowledge in the field of singing, lecturing and spoken word. We are also known for our nurturing, supportive, insightful, enjoyable, holistic, and spiritually encouraging educational pedagogy. Even seasoned singers can achieve an astonishing improvement in their vocal range, vocal health, and vocal power to gain overall resonant balance through this systematic and personally customizable approach. For novice singers, we provide a wonderful opportunity to build a voice free of bad habits. Decades of vocal sessions, with dedication to assisting vocalists, have motivated us to begin offering a greater array of innovative transformational vocal services in the form of retreats and vocal workshops.

Transformational Seminars and Retreats

At our entertaining and enlightening vocal, music, and Performing Arts workshops and seminars, singers are inspired, enlivened, transformed, revitalized, and rejuvenated. Audiences are amazed as vocalists, actors, and speakers make quantum leaps in using their voices. Professional performing artists gain revolutionary insights that help take their performances to a whole new level. Novice singers are transformed into vocalists with full resonance, power, command, symmetry, and balance. In most cases, these transformations occur within a matter of minutes.

The QV Vocal Pedagogy

Regardless of your present vocal style, the QV method will help you master any form of music from pop to opera, or from Christian gospel to esoteric forms of Eastern devotional music. You can upgrade and enhance your voice while you access impressive vocal tonality filled with vibrant clarity and sustained beauty.

Here at QV, we are dedicated to helping you improve your singing and speaking voice. We are devoted to nurturing you, your talent, and your performing artistry. We will help you awaken to a deeper sense of your higher purpose as a vocalist. You can get the support you need to extend your vocal range while you bridge shifts in quality and fix vocal imperfections in an entertaining, engaging, and effortless way.

The QV method is the cornerstone of great singing, utilizing simple terminology to break down complex, in-depth techniques. It will help you achieve and maintain good singing habits and vocal health, as you develop stamina for performing, touring, and for last minute or late night recording sessions. In this easy-to-understand, step-by-step vocal training program, you will learn how to expand your vocal range and how to sing with extraordinary skill, flawless delivery, and inspired expertise.

It's Never Too Late to be Great

Of all the instruments in the world, your voice is the only one you can master at any age. You've been in contact with your vocal instrument from the time you were born and uttered your first sound. Elite athletes normally start out very young, as early as age four, to reach a world-class level of performance.

With the voice, starting out early may have its advantages, but it's never too late to become a great singer. You can obtain vocal grace and proficiency at any stage of life. I call it "vocal plasticity" because it is similar to brain plasticity. You can expand, re-pattern, and retrain the voice at almost any age, just like you can the brain.

A Singer's Bucket List

A woman of advanced years wrote, "Become a Professional Singer", at the top of her Bucket List. She wanted to perform on stage in front of at least 500 people before she departed this world.

"Why did you wait until now?" I asked her.

"When I was a little girl," she said, "a couple of my teachers and family members told me not to sing because I was tone deaf. Broken-hearted, I gave up on following my dream, until one day, I decided to give it another try. I visited five voice teachers. I wasted thousands of dollars, and after no progress I gave up on my dream once again."

She went on to tell me that some years later, a friend told her about my method and my philosophy that if you can talk, you can sing. It is never too late to be great. She felt a renewed enthusiasm for singing and started taking lessons with me. I explained that she would need dedication and would have to hang on my every word. I told her she would need to follow a rigorous schedule just like a world-class athlete in training, including her diet and mindset.

She agreed to the terms. After a few years of dedication and focus, she performed for more than five hundred people at a concert featuring some of the top musicians in the area. At the end of her performance, she received a standing ovation and the crowd was in tears. Her dream of delivering a riveting heartfelt performance had finally come true.

A Diamond in the Rough

When I think about my singing insights and vocal wisdom, it reminds me of what a jeweler does. When she cuts into a rough diamond, she can see just how beautiful the diamond will be in clarity, color, and quality. Using my intuition and vocal acumen, I perceive your voice the same way. All you have to do is sing one note, any note at all, and I can foresee the beauty, resonance, and gem-like quality that will emerge from your voice.

Synergy Between Singing and Speaking

If you want to sing, don't let anything stand in your way. I believe there is no such thing as being tone deaf. Some famous singers have overcome speech impediments to obtain a world-class level of vocal brilliance. Obstacles can be overcome through excitement, love, passion, enthusiasm, and drive to commit to your art. These are the key ingredients. Consistent determination and a daily practice will bring vocal perfection, a formula that applies to all arts, especially the art of living a spiritual life.

Have you ever noticed that a pleasant speaking voice naturally resonates? This natural tonality is the hallmark that indicates how much better a singing voice can sound with expert vocal guidance. The only elements you need are the desire, the focus, a passionate love and dedication to the art.

With this in mind, set aside your fears and concerns. There will be challenges ahead as you embark on becoming a better singer. But if you're willing to face them and persevere, if you're willing to keep pressing forward in spite of your fears, you will ultimately succeed. — Let's begin.

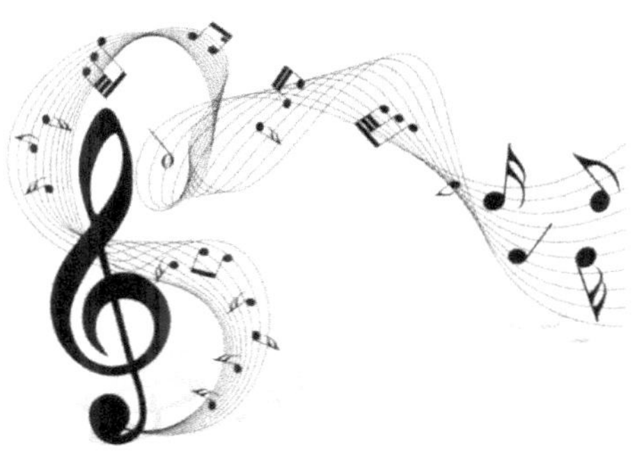

Essentials of Great Singing

Your Signature Sound

What makes your voice unique?

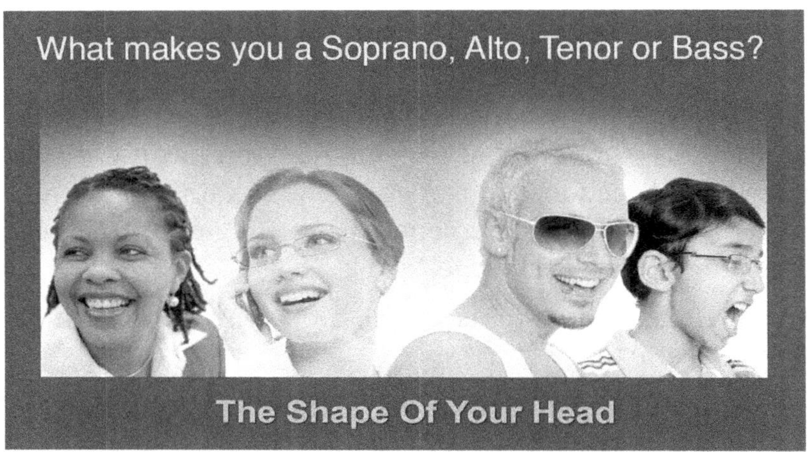

To understand what it takes to be a good singer, it is helpful to understand that we each have a unique voice based on a variety of physical factors. Each singer has a personal resonance to his or her voice. This is why people are altos, tenors, basses, sopranos, or mezzo-sopranos.

What determines the difference in sound, other than gender, is the shape of your head and the passages within, such as the sinus cavities. All these features combined create your own unique tone and captivating sound. Just because your head has a certain shape; however, doesn't mean you'll be a great singer, although with practice and good guidance you can become a great singer at any age. All you need to do is cultivate your sound so that you, as well as others, will find great pleasure in listening to it.

My joyful work is to help you achieve the voice of your dreams, while helping you create what I call a "creative signature sound." This term refers to your own intuitive artistic expression, style, and interpretation of the music. This combination is what will set you apart from everyone else. The development of your creative sound includes cultivating embellishments, various inflections, and stylizations that enhance the beauty, grace, and power of your voice and resonance system. Vocal cultivation and interpretation enrich and develop your artistic portrayal. Overall, it helps create and expand your unique signature sound and your vocal vocabulary.

In seeking to bring out the best in you and your voice, I am offering you the tools, support, and insights that you need. With the right knowledge and direction, you can develop strength, beauty, and vocal balance, as well as creative perception that will help you identify and cultivate your unique vocal niche.

It's time to learn how to use these tools. The first one might surprise you—breathing.

Conscious Breathing

Conscious breathing is necessary in order to measure the correct amount of breath for various phrasings, including sustained resonance and tonal power, to produce a smooth connection and consistency in your vocal sound. In this course, you will learn how ancient yogic breathing techniques can be incorporated to enhance your overall physical, emotional, and spiritual vocal well-being.

Let's start with the *quick breath*. You will need to create the physical sensation of being startled. I suggest a swift intake of air, filling up the lungs quickly, in less than half of your normal breathing time. When you take in air in this manner, it creates suction in the lungs similar to the vacuum effect that occurs when you open a soda can.

The benefit of the quick breath is that it allows for the taking in of the greatest amount of air. This will allow you to sustain notes in a manner that feels and looks effortless. This method of breathing will help expand your lung capacity, allowing you to sing over greater measures of music for longer periods. It is vital to develop the ability to take in air quickly so you don't miss a beat when you're singing long phrases that need fully sustained resonance, tone, and vocal endurance. Remember to keep your face as relaxed and natural as possible so the production looks effortless and natural.

The next step is to learn how to take in a quick breath silently. You have to be careful not to make any sound while inhaling. This seems difficult, but with practice and attention to your intention, everything is possible. Keep your face relaxed while you inhale so you can focus on your bodily expressions and the emotional interpretation of your song. Try to avoid looking like a fish gasping for air, and remember to smile. Your physical appearance will enhance your mood and allow a magical connection with your audience.

Remember, 50 percent of what an audience connects
with is what they see. The rest is what they hear.

With due diligence, this new form of breathing can become second nature. When you're singing, the most effective way to breathe is through the mouth, not the nose. It is very difficult to take in a deep, quick, silent breath through the nose. When you master this form of breathing, you'll be able to focus solely on the intention and artistic expression of the song. Another wonderful aspect of proper breathing is that it helps regulate your tone so the notes stay in tune. You can achieve this by applying steady pressure on the diaphragm in order to sustain resonant quality and tonal balance.

When you exhale during this practice, shape your lips as though you were blowing out of a small straw. This will control and regulate your air as it is being released.

A Good Rule of Thumb:

Whenever you practice vocal exercises, imagine a small spot on the wall in front of you. Funnel all of your air toward that spot as you exhale.

Note: This spot is dynamic. If you are using a blowing motion to get into your higher registers (also called vocal ranges), the spot will remain constantly and directly in your focus. Even when bending or bowing for higher registers, this focus spot remains within your line of vision at all times.

Exercise:

- Inhale and count to ten slowly

- When you inhale, position your mouth as if you're blowing out of a small straw.

- Count to ten again slowly, saying the word "God" or "Om," and keeping a slight pout shape in the mouth for as long as you exhale the breath. This holy sound made with a slight pout, especially on the "d" in the word "God," will give an optimum shape to the mouth.

To get the most out of this exercise, practice it at least five minutes each day until you get the hang of it and the process becomes second nature. Do your best to retain a relaxed state of mind while practicing. Mastering the breath will help the voice when it is fully warmed up to create an amazing effect while you sing over a greater range. It will help you hold longer phrases, giving you a rich tone and allowing for a more compelling vocal performance. Deep breathing has many healthy side effects on the emotional and physiological bodies.

Eighteen Positive Effects of Deep Breathing

Breathing correctly is not only important for living longer, but also for enhancing your mood and allowing you to perform at your best. Let's look at the benefits of deep breathing and why you should make it part of your everyday vocal routine.

1. **Deep Breathing releases toxins**
   Your body is designed to release seventy percent of its toxins through breathing. If you're not breathing effectively, you're not properly ridding your body of toxins. This causes your body to work overtime, which could lead to illness. When you exhale, you release carbon dioxide, a natural waste product of your body's metabolism, from your bloodstream into your lungs.

2. **Deep Breathing releases tension**
   Being anxious, angry, scared, or stressed constricts your breathing. Your muscles get tight, your breathing becomes shallow, and you're not getting the amount of oxygen your body needs.

3. **Deep Breathing relaxes the mind/body and brings clarity**
   Oxygenation of the brain reduces excessive anxiety levels. Breathe slowly deeply, and purposefully into your body. Notice any places that are tight and breathe into them. As you relax your body, you will find that breathing brings you clarity.

4. **Deep Breathing relieves emotional problems**
   Breathing will help clear uneasy feelings out of the body.

5. **Deep Breathing relieves pain**
   Breathing is a direct connection to how you think, feel, and experience life. For example, when you anticipate pain, you probably hold your breath, even though studies show that breathing into your pain helps ease it.

6. **Deep Breathing massages your organs**
    The movements of the diaphragm during deep breathing massages the stomach, small intestine, liver, and pancreas. The upper movement of the diaphragm massages the heart. When you inhale air, your diaphragm descends and your abdomen expands, massaging vital organs and improving circulation. Controlled breathing strengthens and tones your abdominal muscles.

7. **Deep Breathing increases muscle**
    Breathing oxygenates all the cells in your body. With an ample supply of oxygen to your brain and body, muscle mass is increased.

8. **Deep Breathing strengthens the immune system**
    Oxygen travels through your bloodstream by attaching to hemoglobin in your red blood cells. This, in turn, enriches your body's ability to metabolize nutrients and vitamins.

9. **Deep Breathing improves posture**
    Incorrect breathing causes poor body posture. Good breathing techniques practiced over a sustained period of time will encourage good posture. This is an important process. Improving your breathing early on will offer you great benefits.

10. **Deep Breathing improves the quality of your blood**
    Deep breathing removes carbon dioxide and increases oxygen in the blood; thereby, increasing blood quality.

11. **Deep Breathing aids digestion and assimilation of food**
    When the digestive organs receive more oxygen, they operate more efficiently. Digestion is enhanced when your food is more oxygenated.

12. **Deep Breathing improves the nervous system**
    When the brain, spinal cord, and nerves receive increased oxygenation, they are better nourished. This improves your overall health, since the nervous system communicates to all part of the body.

13.   **Deep Breathing strengthens the lungs**
As you breathe deeply, the lungs become healthy and powerful. This is good insurance against respiratory problems.

14.   **Deep Breathing strengthens the heart**
Deep Breathing exercises reduce the workload on the heart in two ways. First, deep breathing leads to more efficient lungs, which means more oxygen is supplied to the blood that is sent to the lungs by the heart. In this way, the heart doesn't have to work as hard to deliver oxygen to the tissues. Second, deep breathing leads to a greater pressure differential in the lungs, which leads to an increase in circulation, which rests the heart.

15.   **Deep Breathing assists with weight control**
If you are overweight, extra oxygen burns up excess fat more efficiently. If you are underweight, the extra oxygen feeds the starving tissue and glands.

16.   **Deep Breathing boosts energy levels and improves stamina**
Deep breathing gives you much more physical energy and can increase your metabolism. When you start breathing properly, you'll have more energy and you'll feel like singing and dancing. Suddenly, you'll find you have the energy and stamina to get the most from life. You may find yourself leaping out of bed in the morning, excited about life. When your cells don't get enough oxygen, they lack the fuel to remove toxins. Since this is one of their major tasks, they tend to get bogged down and are left spinning their wheels, using up whatever fuel is available. Your cells don't give up easily. With proper oxygen, their efforts to get rid of cellular pollution may be more successful. You are only as healthy as your cells. By supplying them with enough oxygen, their job of removing toxic waste is easier and your energy levels will be more consistent. Instead of having highs in the morning and feeling like taking a snooze after lunch, your energy will remain steady during the entire day.

17.   **Deep Breathing improves cellular regeneration**
Proper breathing can restore your health at any age. In ancient times, it was said that deep breathing had a powerful effect. The

Chinese and ancient Indian civilizations developed hundreds of breathing techniques. Now, science has come up to speed with breathing suggestions that increase oxygen and cellular voltage levels, which creates and improves cellular regeneration.

18.   Deep Breathing elevates moods
Breathing is life, so we can expect to feel more alive, vibrant, happier, and healthier through deep breathing. Breathing increases pleasure-inducing neurochemicals in the brain to elevate moods and to combat and heal physical pain. These neurochemicals help dispel depressions, cure insomnia, and reduce anxiety, stress, and emotional irritants. As singers, we get this benefit naturally and feel better in all areas of our lives because deep breathing is essential for our art. When we retrain the way we breathe, we begin to live holistically, because our breath is the most important source of energy.

Hippocrates said, "Air is a pasture of life and the greatest ruler of all." He knew, as did various Oriental philosophers, that the air is "an ocean of energy" ready to be tapped into directly.

Something as simple as breathing can dramatically improve our nation's health and wellbeing. Believe it or not, your breath affects every system in your body (cardiovascular, nervous, endocrine, lymphatic, immune, digestive, and respiratory.) Diaphragmatic breathing is a healthy way to breathe, and it is what we singers do best. It's easy to learn. I've seen people who suffer from asthma, hypertension, anxiety, depression, insomnia, and even chronic pain improve their health dramatically through healthy breathing techniques.

Balanced Breathing

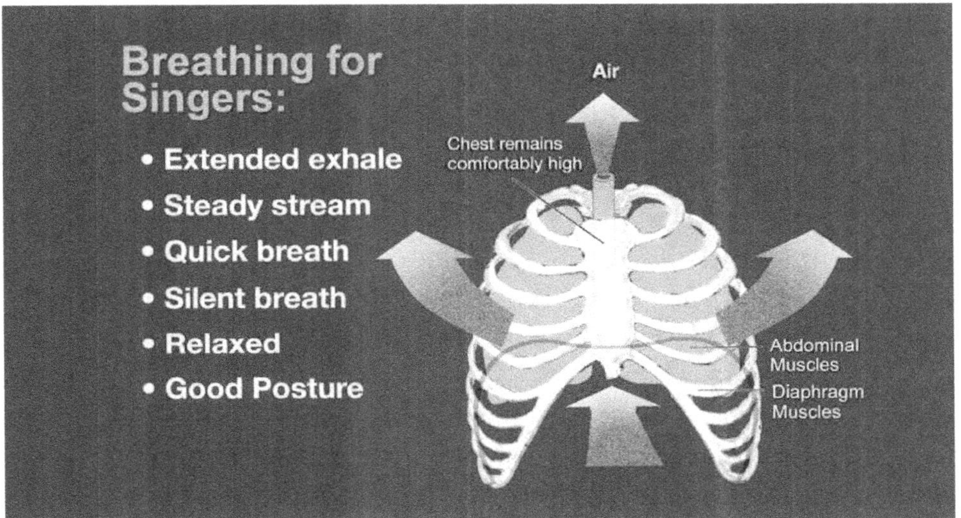

If a singer produces a sound using too much air, the notes will sound breathy. Breathiness, at times, can be a nice embellishment. However, if you use too much air, the voice loses its resonance and fullness, and the sound will be labored. Some forms of music are intentionally sung with a bit of breathiness, since it is the signature of their musical stylization. Breathiness can create interesting flavor, texture, and color, but it must be used as a vocal flare, interwoven within various aspects of the given form of music.

Finding the common denominator is important with airflow and breath control. Doing so will allow you to maintain the foundation of good vocal balance. Mastering the foundation of vocal balance allows a singer to experiment with various forms of vocal flavors, textures, and shades in a way that protects and keeps one's precious singing instrument healthy.

In other words, knowing your healthy vocal balance and center is important. Once you know how it feels and sounds to produce notes correctly, you will have greater vocal freedom. Then, you can experiment to experience a creativity that comes from infusing intuitive improvisations with tasty embellishments. This creative process will teach you how to blend vocal flavors, textures, and shades in order to create your signature sound.

Breathing With Intention

In order to breathe with intention, you need to breathe deeply into your abdomen as well as your chest. In ancient Greece and Rome, doctors recommended deep breathing, the voluntary holding of air in the lungs. They believed that this exercise cleansed the system of impurities and developed strength. Breathing exercises should be through the nose and mouth. The breaths must be deep, slow, and rhythmic. When singing; however, it is best to breathe through the mouth.

For singers, the most important part of breathing is regulating the breath. In order to expand your lung capacity, the breath must be sustained. This can be accomplished by holding the breath for four counts in and four counts out. Another method you can use for lung expansion and its health benefits is Pranayama Yoga breathing.

Here is an example of a deep-breathing exercise taken from Pranayama Yoga:

1. Inhale through your nose, expanding your belly, and then fill your chest, counting to five.

2. Hold and count to three. Feel your cells fill up with golden, healing sunlight energy.

3. Exhale fully out of the mouth as you count to five. Feel all of your cells releasing waste and emptying old and unfavorable energy.

The first step in mastering stress is to honor yourself by scheduling time for self-care and spiritual artistic development. Schedule your deep breathing exercises just as you would schedule important business appointments. Tending to your relationships with the self, the inner artist, the material, and spiritual bodies, will heighten your relationship with life and with God. This will flow over into your relationships with the world around you, enriching and deepening all aspects of your life. Once you obtain a beautiful, resonant angelic voice share it with your children, friends, loved ones, and especially with the Lord of all. Let everyone enjoy the immense benefits with you.

Singing: A Divine Intuitive Process

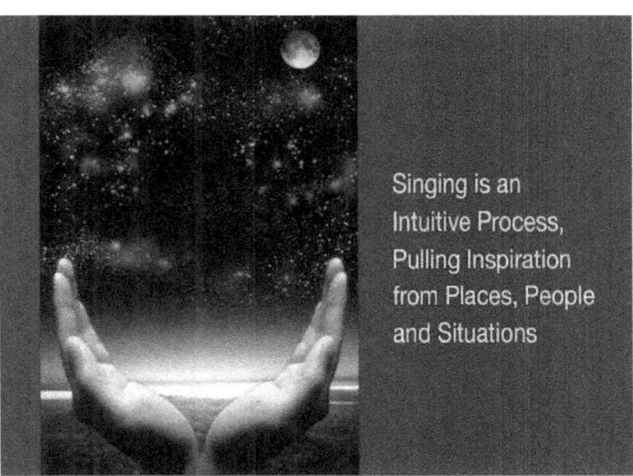

As singers, speakers, actors, and artists, we pull inspiration from the world around us. This includes our environment, our experiences, and the spiritual traditions we follow. Our inspiration is filtered through our own creative expression. For many of us, our greatest creative inspiration, that which ignites the muse within, comes from having a spiritual belief system. When we tune into something higher than ourselves—that which is divine in nature—we meet the catalyst that brings forth the most captivating and beautiful art from the core of one's heart.

In my experience, the highest and most inspiring use of your voice is singing for the Lord of all love, including the saints and angels. No matter what you call God, whether it's Lord Jesus, Sri Krishna, Lord Buddha, Sri Rama, Allah, or Jehovah, all of His names are imbued with mystical, transcendental qualities. Keeping His name as your constant companion brings all goodness to life. Being an advocate of religious tolerance, I see this as being one of the most essential keys to global harmony. Infusing this concept, when a sincere and devout intention is held fast in the mind of the vocalist, spiritual inspiration and healing flows into the hearts and souls of the listeners.

Accessing the Creative Process

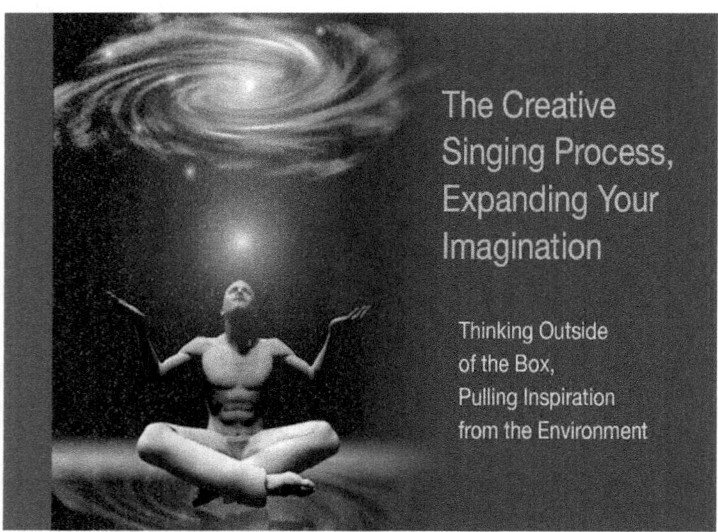

Besides mastering vocal techniques, a singer's performance is affected by these higher forms of inspiration. This inspiration leads to the singer's intuitive interpretation of a song. The singer must learn to tap into his or her inner listening. Albert Einstein came up with some of his greatest theories while he was relaxing and playing his violin, a spontaneous, intentional tuning to the higher planes of creative existence, a process similar to transcendental meditation.

Have you ever watched an actor get into character? He or she tunes into past and present experiences, capturing the mood and inner frame of emotions. An actor instinctively conjures up a particular sentiment by allowing it to well up from the depths of the soul, then letting it overflow into their artistic expression. This expression gives the actor the ability to deliver an authentic, natural, and captivating performance. These emotions, ideas, and insights are the foundation of artistic expression in the performing arts world. As aspiring spiritual artists, these forms of expression come from a higher plane of understanding.

As a singer, you will encompass and personify these same artistic attributes, capturing the emotions flowing from the inner most regions of your heart's emotions. Drawing upon these forms of intuitive impressions and expression, helps you deliver captivating vocal masterpieces when you perform.

This inner knowledge and understanding creates the magic needed for a compelling and inspiring performance. However, when these same principles are adapted to a more consecrated spiritual format, the effect defies explanation. It takes you and the listener to profound higher astrospheres. Therefore, before you sing, take a moment to listen, to tune into the heart of the song, to ponder the mood, and to meditate on the deeper meaning and message. Make sure the songs you choose make you feel alive and are spiritually soul stirring. This stillness is similar to contemplation—the place where you can enter into the soul of the song.

Within this mindset, you will be able to absorb and embody the sentiment of the music with your heart and then disseminate it into the hearts of others. The expression you are seeking to convey with your voice will come into full resonant beauty with keeping these simple yet profound concepts in focus.

In this intuitive stillness, you can capture the inner meaning and embody the emotion of your song. It is my belief that the highest form of singing comes from the core of one's soul. To achieve this, you must sing as if each note was the most precious jewel from your inner heart, a priceless gift given with such tenderhearted love, to the Creator of All Universes, the ocean of compassion. Then your mood will reflect the essence of these holy realms. With this in mind, your performance has the power to illuminate the minds of millions. This mood is a reflection of God's heavenly light, which can help save the human race. Therefore, your voice can heal shattered hearts, mend splintered minds, bring a spirit back to life, and give wholeness and strength to a weakened soul. This is the essence of sacred singing—it allows miracles to take place.

Divine songs are so powerful that they pass the subtle mind and enter directly into the heart of your soul's consciousness. Here, the spirit can experience the euphoric ecstasy of spiritual rhapsody. This is the greatest gift that you as a transformational vocal artist can give others.

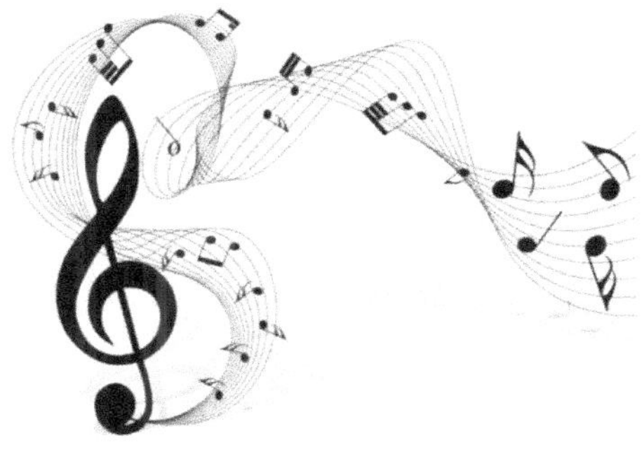

Your Vocal Anatomy

Your Divine Instrument

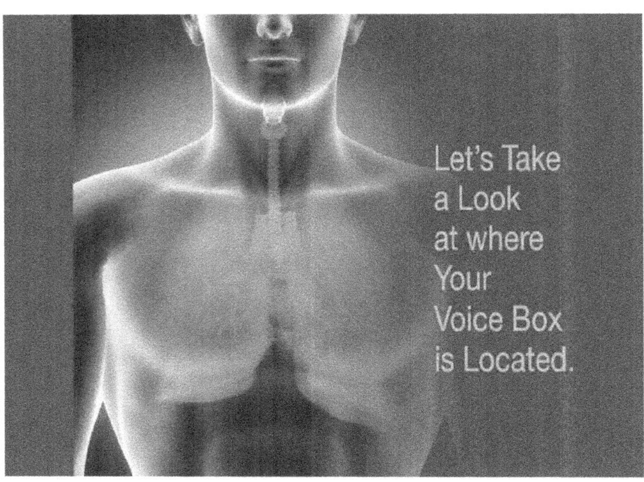

The image above indicates where your sacred vocal box is located. Although we all use our voices when we're talking and singing, most of us don't actually know where it is positioned. This diagram helps give a more comprehensive understanding of your wonderful God-given instrument.

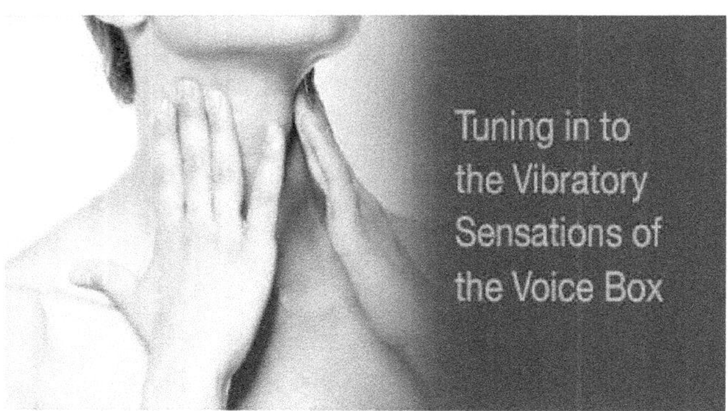

To locate your voice box, place your hands halfway between the collarbone and chin, as shown in the image above. Repeat the words God, God, God, or Om, Om, Om, in a relaxed tone, with a lightly pouty shape to your mouth. Choose any note that comes easily and naturally. This will allow you to feel the position of the vibrations caused by the tone of the word. For men, it's easy to locate, because it's behind the Adam's apple.

The words, "God" and "Om" are aerodynamically structured so you can naturally create the sounds with the optimum-shaped embouchure (shape of your mouth). Uttering the words "God" or "Om" helps to eliminate strain on your vocal instrument. Remember to add the slight pout as it helps to retain the aerodynamic shape that facilitates a healthy, relaxed tone. Also, these two words cross over religious barriers, as they are transcendent and universal. "God" and "Om" are two of the most beneficial sounds for one's daily practice.

Note: The voice box seems intangible, since it cannot be seen. However, understanding the vocal anatomy is essential. This is why it is important to locate your voice box. Over time, you will become proficient at maneuvering the instrument until the motion becomes seamless. The internal and external recognition of your voice is utterly vital to your vocal progress.

To master the voice is to understand and apply the mental memorization of the physical sensations, while at the same time, implementing the vocal method correctly. This means that you know how it sounds and how it feels when you are singing. It should feel effortless and sound-balanced when you're in the right vocal zone.

Singing is Dancing with Your Voice

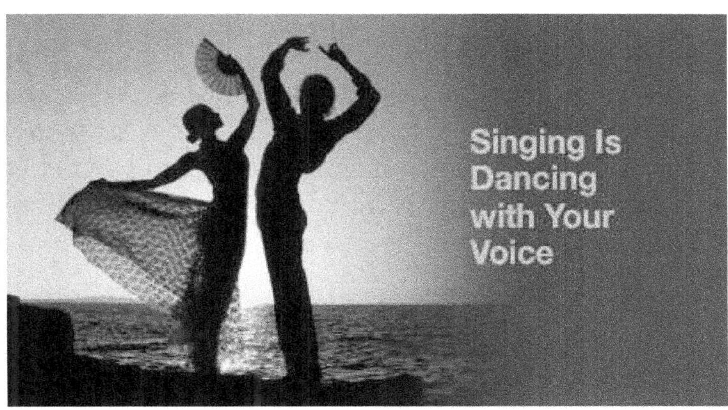

Being a dancer from age five, I discovered the parallel between singing and dancing. When a dancer performs, he or she no longer has the mirror used in practice to spot-check postures or positions. Dancers have to rely on memorizing physical sensations in order to replicate the choreography. This process allows the performer to deliver the performance with poise, elegance, agility and balance.

Just like dancers, we singers can't see our instrument. We have to rely on the memory of physical sensations in order to keep our voices in balance and hold the controlled internal vocal postures needed to sing with clarity and agility. When you become proficient at recalling these internal postures and aligning your movements, your sound will be on mark, in tune, melodious and your learning curve will accelerate.

How do you know whether you're singing with the proper vocal balance or in the vocal mix (what some call the "vocal zone")? For that matter, how do you know whether you're singing in tune, or what muscles to use to maneuver and navigate the vocal range? Also, what is the formula to know whether you have attained the perfect vocal amalgamation needed to sing with optimum effectiveness and natural resonance?

The answer is simple, applying the exercises and vocal mapping found here within, combined with the unusual sounds prescribed are the key and will bring about the vocal balance, strength and agility needed to create the vocal symmetry desired. These unorthodox exercises will warm up, strengthen, and stretch your vocal muscles, a kind of heavy lifting for your voice.

These unusual sounds have an effect on a singer similar to the way dancers warm up their bodies before doing exercises and choreography. These seemingly eccentric vocal exercises and sounds help identify the various parts of the voice, while offering agility and building up power and stamina in your vocal instrument. Then you can identify the parts of your voice that access, engage, and isolate the correct muscles while performing or warming up.

A Rule of Thumb:

It is important to understand and identify the correct areas within the vocal apparatus to activate the areas used to sing properly. The ability to isolate the areas designated for chewing and swallowing is beneficial, something we will discuss later.

When singing up into the head voice, known as the higher ranges, it is important to sing correctly. If you are singing improperly, you'll feel compression or strain in and around the voice box. The notes will become strident and labored. At times, the notes can flip up into the next note, often referred to as "the next room." These occurrences, if not corrected, can cause vocal impairment, so it's best to learn the correct way to sing as early as possible.

Internal Memorization

I'd like to elaborate on the physiological sensations of singing. In order to implement the correct singing formula, you must master the ability to sustain various postures internally. For example, when a pianist is holding a chord by pressing down the keys with his fingers, he is creating the sustained sound with his fingers in that particular position. Singing is essentially the same, but a bit more esoteric, because you can't see the instrument. You are sustaining internal postures that are dynamic in nature and you are modifying them according to placement in the range and the desired lyrical effect.

This aspect of singing is comparable to dancing. When dancers are starting out, they have a mirror to spot-check their postures. For singers, the vocal mirror is an expert vocal coach, someone who can provide accurate feedback with intuitive precision. If you don't have access to a vocal coach, try looking on-line. If need be, you can act as your own coach, by recording yourself and listening back, in order to evaluate your practice session.

I find it best to have a minimum of four lessons with a good intuitive vocal coach. Make sure they can do the exercises properly and can demonstrate them to you. They must be able to process your sounds through the filter of their own ear so they can provide an accurate analysis of your vocal needs. They must be able to detect whether or not your notes contain symmetry, are melodious and harmonically resonate with nature.

In other words, an expert coach makes sure the sound is not sharp or flat, and spot-checks for compression so the sound is not pushed prematurely into the higher ranges. This is an all too common mistake made by many singers. Adept guidance gives you the vocal support and fortitude to sing with charisma, mastery and spiritual conviction. This results in a healthy vocal approach that will protect your precious vocal instrument for the rest of your life.

Another analogy between dancing and singing is posture. Dancers must maintain good posture so they don't lose balance. They must demonstrate a visually captivating presence to the audience. Singers also need to sustain good posture in order to produce a vibrant sound and give a compelling performance. A singer needs to have mastery over the process in order to sustain a vocal acumen that is finely tuned and calibrated.

The Dynamics of Balancing Air and Muscle

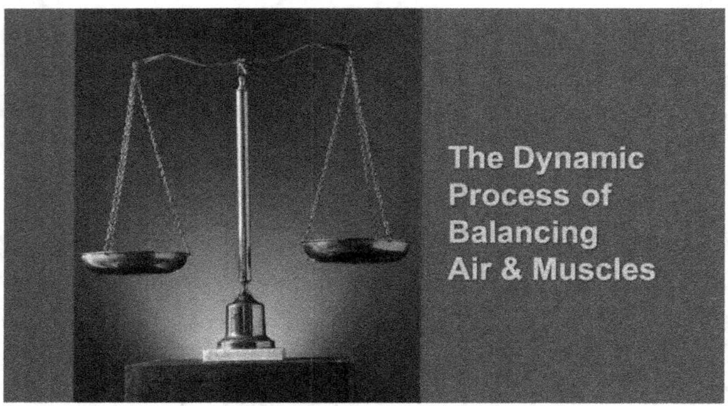

Let's look at the intrinsic interaction and balance of the dance that takes place between your airflow and your muscles. This interaction and balance helps you to create and maintain your internal vocal choreography. Once you can grasp the somewhat abstract concept of how to properly maneuver these areas of your vocal apparatus and implement them with accuracy, your voice will be freed of all impediments. Then, you can achieve the balance of air and muscles, and you will not be at risk of vocal dysfunction or downtime. In this way, the Quantum Vocalist method can rehabilitate and revitalize voices that have sustained abnormalities due to less than desirable habits or methods.

Normally, undesirable vocal habits are the result of exposure to poor vocal techniques and/or the lack of expert guidance. In these circumstances, irregularities surface particularly when a singer goes into a head voice, also known as the upper vocal registers. Singing higher and louder is often difficult for singers, especially if they have not had access to a good vocal method such as QV. Without adequate training, chances of abnormalities appearing in your voice escalate.

To prevent this, it is imperative to master the balance of air and muscle. For instance, you may sing a note and unknowingly compress into it. If the note is not properly sustained, with the correct internal postures, that area will tend to shift in quality. This is known as a break in the range and you will find it more difficult to sing with a robust resonance.

Many singers, even professionals who come to me, are using too many muscles, particularly when they traverse into the upper registers. This makes their sounds labored, discordant and stressed, giving way to vocal dysfunction. This happens because the voice box, if not trained properly, will instinctively try to hold the air back, constricting the muscles and causing imbalances in the voice.

If this practice is not spot-checked by an expert vocal coach with an educated, intuitive ear, these kinds of imbalances can cause vocal impairment. This possibility underscores the need to be fully absorbed into these vocal concepts under expert guidance in order to have a voice that is buoyant, animated and endowed with fascinating, heavenly attributes.

The Internal Listening Process

Listening attentively to music in a similar range or style to your own is as important as singing. Listening is a form of audio memorization and visualization that helps you create a vivid mental concept of what you would like to emulate in your performance. I feel it is vitally important to wrap your mind around inspiring, uplifting and positive spiritual music regularly, because engaging in an activity repetitively is a proven method of brain reprogramming. Repetitive sounds are a type of affirmation that helps train your brain to manifest these concepts in your life.

Films or books like *What the Bleep Do We Know?*, *The Secret*, and *The Power of I Am*, are based on your thoughts. When you read or watch something inspiring, your life will be filled with wonderful experiences. Since most of life's journey is an internal emotional experience, bliss and happiness are only a thought away.

I suggest you fill your life with divine purpose and amazing enlightening experiences that create a vivid inner world. If you integrate the reality of God Consciousness, there are no impossible problems in life because, you can solve them with faith. However, since each person is unique, whatever it takes to make you feel great and connected to the Infinite of All is your brightest path. Regardless of what is happening around you, one can always make the decision to be happy, peaceful and content. This is the higher road of conscious living that translates into a life of inner transformation, as well as emotional and physical health, and longevity.

Since the brain doesn't know what is happening to you in the external world, you can simply say to yourself with kindness and conviction: *I am feeling great, happy, blissful, grateful, blessed, healthy, whole, content, inspired, and sublimely focused on having my best life now.* It works.

Magically, your brain will go along with the program, particularly if the intention and tone of your inner voice reflect compassion and certainty. Your positive voice, both external and internal, is so powerful that it will override negativity and create an instantaneous elevation in mood. Mastering the voice is a great way to start.

Another way to make needed emotional shifts is to combine positive internal affirmations with slow, deep breathing and prayers. The result will be nothing short of remarkable, because this prayerful state will accelerate the shift and help your body, mind and spirit to thrive. You will experience a lighthearted and healthier you. It will help reduce stress, anxiety, irritation, anger and depression, which actually shrink the brain like a raisin!

Exploring the Vocal Matrix

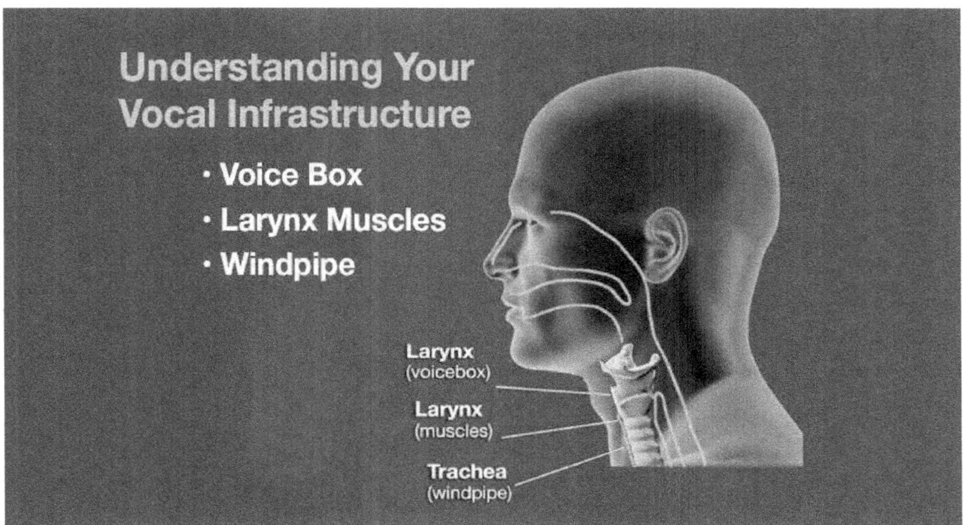

This diagram demonstrates the internal structure of your voice. It shows where the voice box is located, and it also displays the soft palate area and resonance system used to create a beautiful reverberation within your vocal instrument.

Here, we are focusing on the trachea, also known as the windpipe, which has a big job carrying air from the lungs. It picks up notes from the voice box and sends them out of the mouth in one fluid movement. This is where the magic of singing takes place.

Your Vocal Anatomy

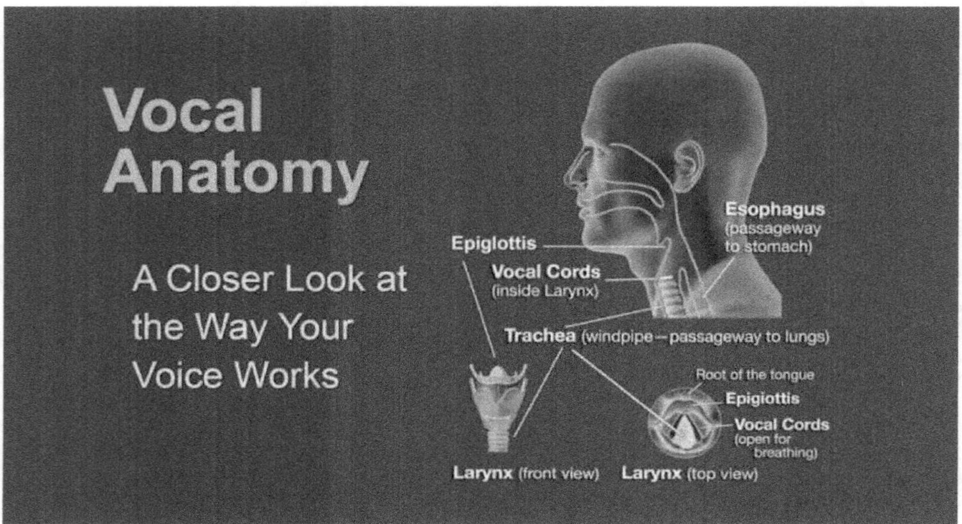

The following practice will help you replicate your internal vocal postures more spontaneously. To be great at singing takes practice, so the trick is to *fully concentrate*. This is called "intentional practice." Concentrated practice, the secret formula to excelling and achieving a world-class level of singing, is the optimal way to make steady improvement. This is particularly true under the guidance of an expert intuitive vocal coach. It takes due diligence to allow your vocal instrument to develop into the higher echelon of vocal equilibrium attainment. Practice, dedication, passion and love of singing make for clear vocal perfection.

World-class singers, like world-class athletes, are always looking for ways to improve their art. They always practice with this mindset and will search out a seasoned coach with whom they resonate. To obtain higher levels of vocal perfection, vocalists pay attention and avoid automatic modes of practice so they don't fall into mechanical routines. This kind of intentional concentration opens the student to greater Improvement. *The diligent student is eager to get feedback from a vocal coach to make lasting improvement.*

The key to having an intelligent practice is combining intentional focus with feedback from your vocal coach. A student who hangs on a coach's every word, and takes those words to heart, is much more likely to achieve his or her vocal dream, no matter how lofty. If you have read this far, you are a singer at heart. Drinking in and hanging on every word about the Quantum Vocalist Method will bring you closer to your goal of vocal refinement and perfection. Through this process, practicing will no longer be a laborious task, but rather a soul-rewarding experience.

CHAPTER THREE

Vocal Mapping

The Three Voices

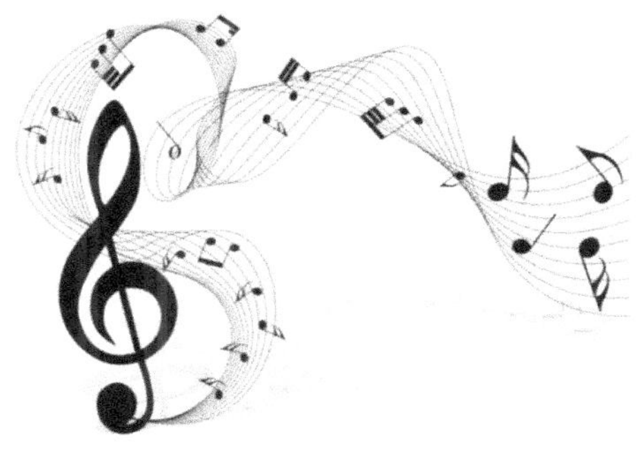

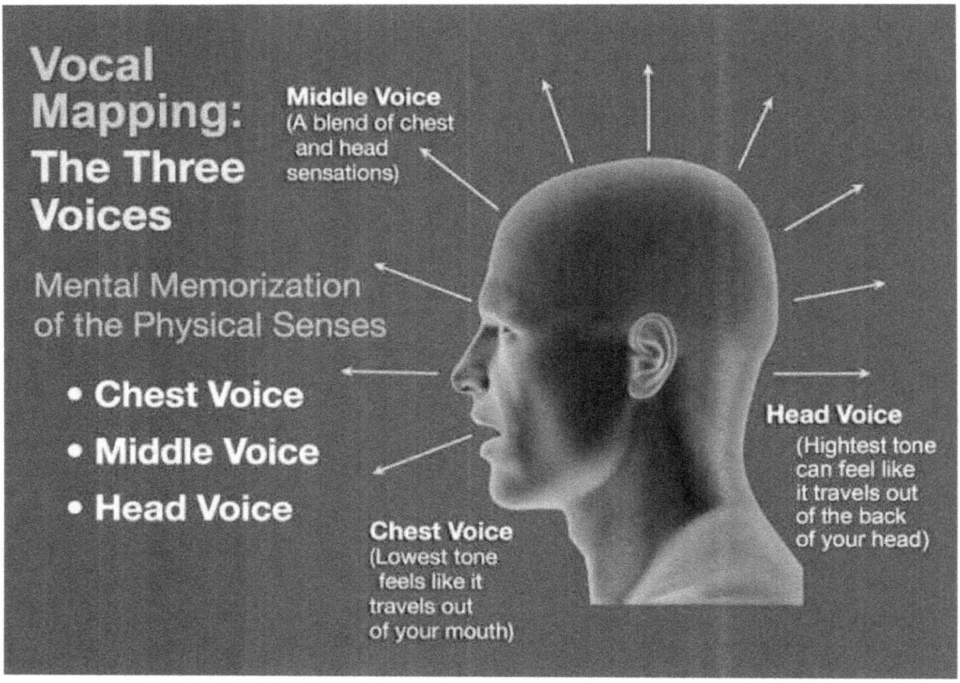

It is vitally important to understand the voice's mapping process, also known as "singing through the three voices." Regardless of music style, this is something all singers have to master.

The three voices include:

- Chest voice: the lower register

- Middle voice: the blend of both the head and the chest

- Head voice: the high registers

It doesn't matter what genre of music you are singing. It might be gospel, inspirational, rock, pop, devotional or opera. In each case, mastering the three voices is essential.

Have you ever heard the expression: *She was a master of three voices?*

This generally refers to opera singers, but all singers must become proficient in getting through these areas. The diagram above shows the approximate vocal regions.

The easiest way to find these areas is to sing the note in that particular range, starting with the chest voice. Depending on your range, this tone is usually a note located below the middle C. Once you play this random note on the keyboard, sing the syllable, "Ra" or "Om", with a slight pout to your mouth. Then, place your hand on your chest so you can feel the sound traveling out of that part of your body.

The next voice, the middle voice, is located higher up the scale. It is generally found just above the middle C, depending on your range. When you play the note and sing the syllable "Ra" or "Om," again and you will feel like the sound is coming out of the mask of your face.

Finally, to find the head voice, play a note that is around the A, A# or B, just above middle C, depending on your range. For men, you will normally sing an octave down. Place your hand above your forehead while again singing the syllable "Ra" or "Om." You can experience the sound traveling out of the front and top of your head. To avoid vocal strain, add in a deep frontal bow before you sing a higher note, especially when you start to feel compression.

Many times, even seasoned singers will have a tendency to sing the note in the wrong voice, causing them to overshoot or overreach for the note. When we speak about overshooting or overreaching, it means that the note should have been placed lower into the middle or chest voice. When a singer overshoots a note, he or she has prematurely pushed the note into the upper registers. If a singer sings a note and overshoots it, the note will sound compressed, strained, light or pitchy in resonance.

The sound of a note produced in this way is unhealthy due to the improper placement. If a singer is trying to belt out a note, while at the same time, is "reaching for the note," she will eventually experience deep vocal fatigue. When the outer larynx muscles compress around the voice box in the overreaching posture, the resonant tones can't take place because the sound is being dampened by the muscular compression.

However, if we simply bring that note down into the right position, the sound will once again be beautiful, full and bright. The note will be produced easily and sung effortlessly.

When the note is positioned correctly, it is not only produced effortlessly, but you can hear and experience all the wonderful harmonic tones present in each note, simply by applying the theory of vocal mapping. The same analogy can be applied to life. When you find the harmonic balance in life, you can live effortlessly.

Sustaining Vocal Postures

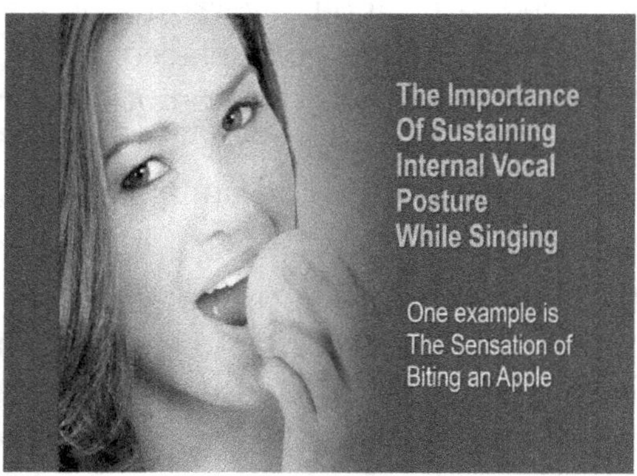

The physical sensation of biting into an apple is a simple act that provides insight into another physical sensation that is useful in singing. This internal movement helps you locate the upper larynx region, an area that has a tendency to hike up into the head voice when you're singing.

Imagine you're about to take a bite of an apple. Close your eyes and make a mental note of how it feels to perform this internal movement. You will feel the gentle, downward movement of the upper larynx muscles. This movement creates the needed space to sing over the soft palate area and into the higher vocal regions. This internal posture is called the "humble angel." (Some circles call it the dumb sound, but the QV method doesn't like to reinforce negative affirmations or mindsets in its curriculum. Studies show that positive learning methods provide results up to 75 percent faster than negative ones.)

Think about this internal muscular shift in terms of making a primitive sound like "ugh." A Neanderthal might have sounded like this. Remember to stay relaxed internally while generating this sound. While making this sound, the internal larynx muscles are being shifted in a downward motion. This movement helps strengthen and stretch those muscles while repositioning them correctly. When this happens, you can sing up over the soft palate area and enter more easily into the upper ranges. This repositioning will help you to establish an effortless, painless and damage-free form of singing.

When you practice the exercises designed to help your particular set of needs, you can achieve greater vocal command, influence and presence. The key to unlocking the power of this method is the repetition of the exercises. You can find this on the QV website for free. In time, all of these heady concepts will come together synergistically and will be second nature for you. This is all a part of creating strength and flexibility, as well as having the ability to sustain vocal postures.

Effortless Singing

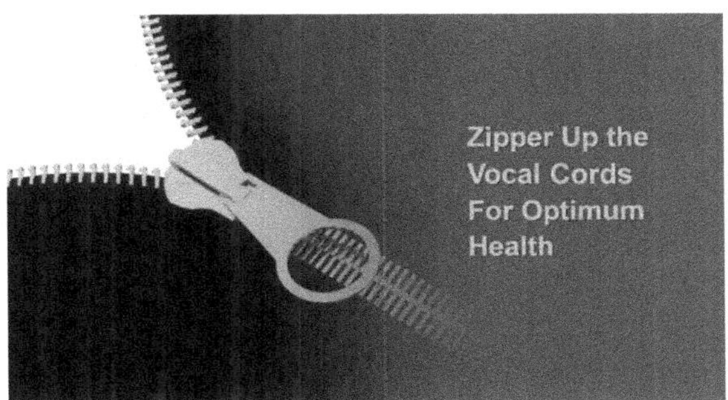

The image above is an example of what happens internally when you use the sound of a light edgy cry, or what we call the "edgy angel." This important application comes into play when you're singing in the higher vocal ranges. Some people refer to this as the "zipping up" of the vocal chords, although the sound is similar to a lightly creaking door rather than a zipper. The key is that the sound must be produced in a relaxed vocal state. No compression is to be felt around the voice box.

It sounds like "ahhhhhh." Internally, the vocal chords are gently zippering them together from the back to the front of the voice box. This application is most needed when singing into the higher vocal ranges, since singing higher can be harder. You can view samples of this on our web site for free. As with life, the more challenging things become, the more effort and determination are needed.

This function is important in voice training, because it helps preserve vocal health, especially while traversing the three voices or belting out notes. I like to use the analogy of a balloon to describe what happens when zippering up the vocal chords.

Imagine filling up a balloon with air. Now, take the mouth of the balloon and stretch it out. Next, very slowly bring the corners of the balloon back together. The sound that emanates is very loud and very high in pitch. When you master zippering up the vocal chords with the edgy angel sound, the vocal chords will emulate a balloon being stretched, and the air slowly being released. Note: It does not take more air to create a higher, louder sound. However, it does take more air pressure built up behind the vocal chords.

Zippering up the vocal chords with the edgy angel, without compression, pulls the chords together and creates the needed pressure behind them. This allows the singer to belt into the vocal breaks effortlessly, as well as sing in the higher registers that are normally more difficult to sing into.

The breaks or shifts occurring in your vocal quality normally starts from the middle ranges on up. The areas are the A, A# and B, just above middle C, and then again around the D, D# and E, depending on your range. I will discuss this subject more in depth later. As these areas are known to cause singers the most trouble, it is essential to be attentive to mastering these shifts in quality in order to get a good vocal blending throughout your range.

The edgy angel, combined with other vocal tools, will create the sound bridge needed to produce a smooth, powerful connection in your overall vocal sound as you journey through the three voices.

This smooth sound is what we call singing in the vocal zone or the "vocal mix." With the blending of muscular postures in the activation and deactivation processes, you can achieve the ability to belt in the blend to such a degree, that your voice can effortlessly fill up a large concert hall.

Now that you understand how vocal mapping works, in the next chapter, I'll show you how you can use the shape of your mouth to improve your sound and tone.

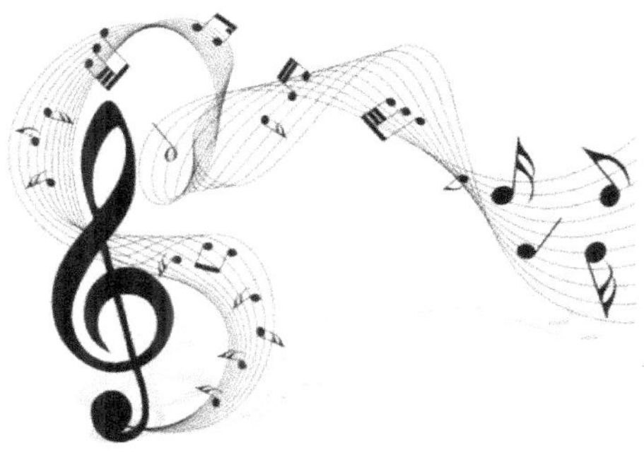

CHAPTER FOUR

The Vocal Embouchure

The Angel Mouth

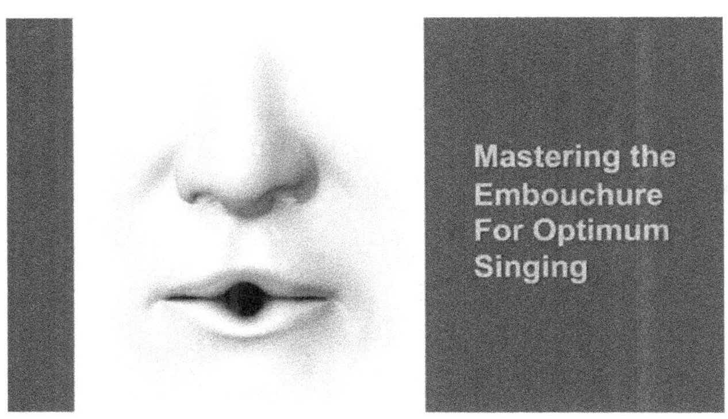

The *embouchure*, also known as the shape of your mouth, needs to be situated so you can produce the perfect, resonant tone. This shape is aerodynamic in nature and allows a full, rich, healthy and more robust sounding tone. It helps to sustain long-term vocal endurance and fitness.

In the image above, the shape of the mouth can be compared to the bell or mouth of a horn. Imagine a horn maker creating a top-of-the-line horn. He will pay special attention to the bell's circumference because a fraction of a millimeter in variation can alter the horn's sound. This concept also holds true for a singer's mouth.

You might hear professional singers splatting their vowels. This splatting sound happens when the circumference of the mouth is open horizontally to a wide degree, similar to a wide smile. The result is the delivery of an imperfectly shaped embouchure. This flaw will eventually take its toll on a singer's voice and can lead to vocal damage. The tone can be strident and pale in production.

You can notice a dramatic difference in overall tonality when you're listening to a singer who has mastered the angel's mouth. Why do I call it the "angel's mouth"? Can you remember seeing a picture of a group of angels singing in a choir around Christmas time? They all have this oval shaped mouth. I like to refer to this position as the "angels mouth, because I like to wrap my consciousness and that of my students around the highest and most positive affirmations.

In order to achieve the perfected angel-shaped mouth, take two fingers, line them up vertically, and then place them in your mouth. This will give your mouth the more optimal shape. This narrowed embouchure is important because ninety percent of words in most languages have a tendency to splat. For example, the words "way, "they," "these" and "that," have this horizontal formation. If you say these words in front of a mirror, you can see a horizontal shape that, if not corrected, can cause vocal fatigue and disorder.

The Angel Mouth in Action

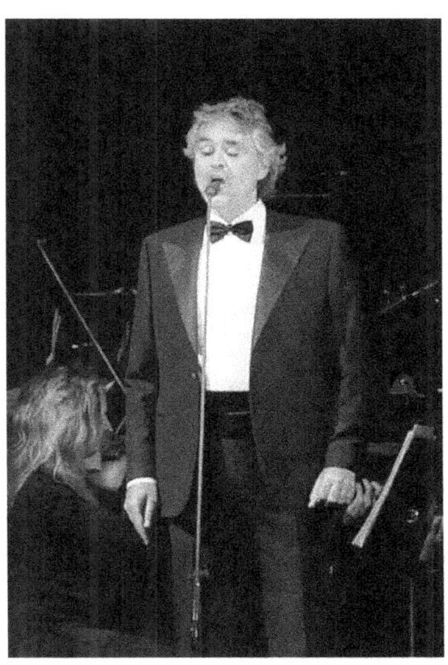

Legendary opera singer, Andrea Bocelli, is a master of the angel mouth. Because of his blindness, the rest of his senses have become heightened, giving him a stellar ear that is acutely tuned into the sound of his own voice. The angel's mouth is second nature to him, which is one of the reasons he is able to produce such captivating, resonant tones. The long-term beneficial result of mastering the angel's mouth is that the voice is wonderfully maintained and has radiant health, even into one's golden years.

The Benefits of the Vocal Yawn

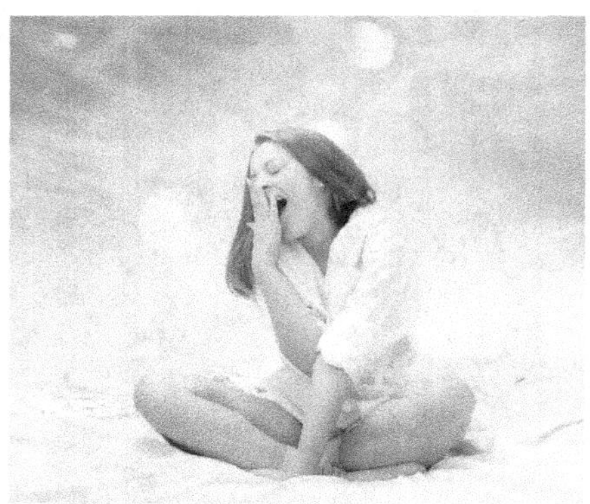

The internal movement of the vocal yawn is an important element. This posture helps to release the outside larynx's muscular compression. These muscles tend to tighten in and around the voice box and shove the sound upward, particularly into the head voice when you're belting notes. The yawn eases the tension by gently pushing downward against this tendency, helping you release the unnecessary muscle tension, thus allowing the vocalist to sing higher into the head voice with greater ease.

When you need to get through difficult times, constant recalibration of your mind to dwell in the higher octaves of understanding is needed. It is the same with the yawning movement, an especially helpful internal movement, because most singers have a tendency to engage the outside larynx muscles when singing into higher voices.

At times, this group of muscles get activated when singing; however, they should only be used in the chewing and swallowing process, not the singing process. If we use this group of muscles when we're singing, it creates a laborious and arduous sound. The QV method helps you to identify these muscles so you can isolate them. This all-important isolation is encouraged with a slight yawn. When applied while singing, it results in resonant tonality and helps to extend the vocal longevity. However, this yawn must be combined with the other forms of internal vocal maneuvers and postures previously discussed and prescribed. These combined techniques enable you to navigate the vocal range, while maintaining the agility to sustain overall singing ease.

Connecting to the Speaking Voice

The benefit of mastering the physical sensations and tones associated with the various notes is that it helps you to avoid inadvertently placing the note in the wrong register.

A quick way to resolve this issue is to start speaking the lyrics as if you were reading from a theatrical script. Remember to relax as you speak, and bring your awareness to your sound, so you can connect with the emotional voice of your soul. This process will align you with the natural placement of your tone, bringing the voice back into the right register. The result will naturally create a more comfortable sound production.

Easing Vocal Compression: The Yoga Lion

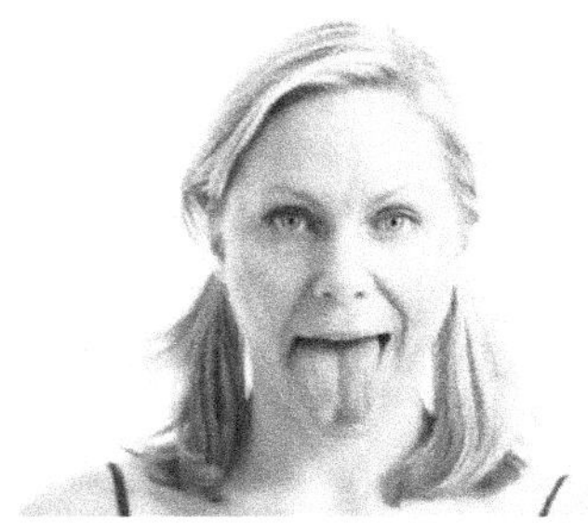

The yoga lion pose (also known as the tongue stretch) is very useful whenever you feel the soft palate rise in the back of the throat. As this rise will cut off or muffle your resonance. The lion pose is the best way to reduce the compression and situate your internal vocal postures elsewhere. Now all you need to do is gently extend your tongue as if you were trying to touch the ground with it, staying as relaxed as possible while doing so. If you want to be daintier in this application, put your hand over your mouth so others cannot view the tongue in this position.

Make the sound "aww," while producing a melodic phrase will help you readjust the tonality. It is important to stay as relaxed as possible to release all compression and open up the soft palate area quickly. Once you've done this a few times, immediately sing the melody using the lyrics that you were struggling with. You will find an amazing, renewed balance in your sound. It is best to practice this exercise for a few minutes each day until the tongue is retrained.

Maximizing Your Resonant Sound

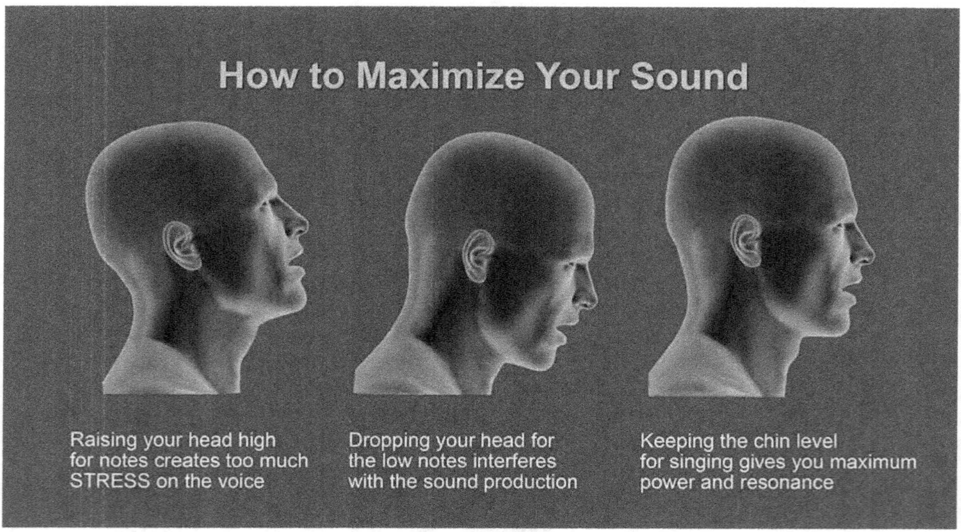

The above image shows the incorrect and correct head positions for the chest, middle and head voices. Many singers have a tendency to lift their heads when they're singing high notes or to drop their chins when they're singing low notes. However, both of these actions will cause the voice to wedge up after a period of time due to it being an unhealthy posture for the voice. You might see professional singers using incorrect head positions, but eventually such positioning will catch up with them. Young singers can get away with using less than optimum head postures, but after a while, especially as the body ages, it will ultimately cause vocal impairment.

When you start becoming sensitive and more intuitive to the various physical sensations taking place in your singing apparatus, you'll notice that incorrect positions add strain, and causing wear and tear on the voice.

Here is a good example: Imagine a garden hose. If you put a crimp in the hose, it will diminish the flow of water. Similarly, when singers are trying to sing low or high notes, and use postures that add strain or too much bend to the windpipe, it will constrict the airflow and decrease the overall tonality, just like in the garden hose.

Whether you're practicing or performing, a singer needs to keep their chin relatively level to allow for maximum airflow and tonality. You can still incorporate interpretive gestures, movements and facial expressions in order to embody the mood of your song in lyrical choreography. However, it is best done within the context of proper vocal posture in relation to the music. The most important thing to remember is to keep your body in a relatively correct posture at all times.

The Vocal Funnel Sound Focus

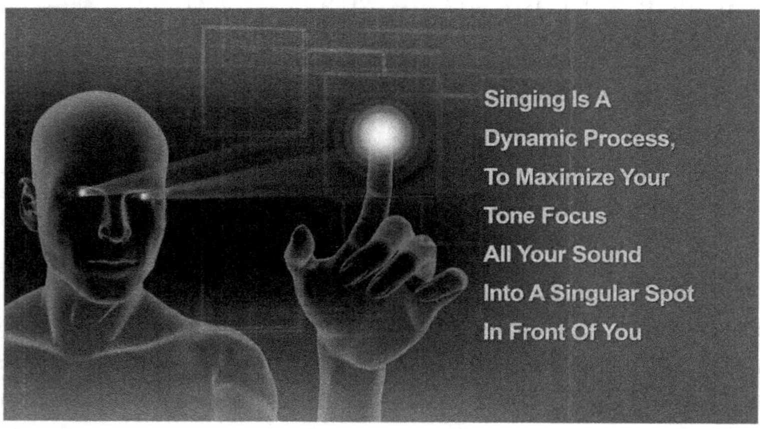

When singing, make sure your sound is focused. To do this, visualize a small spot in front of you and funnel all of your sound into it. Imagine that you're blowing a feather in the air with a steady stream of breath, trying to keep the feather afloat. Another visual technique is to imagine an invisible golden cord that goes from your mouth to the wall in front of you. Visualize your notes being carried by your breath and surfing along this golden cord to that imaginary spot. Since that spot is dynamic in nature, wherever your body moves, the spot moves with you. When moving your body around while performing, this spot is going to be a consistent focus of your sound.

When utilizing the vocal positions discussed in this chapter, you'll experience a greater ease in singing, as you will be in the "vocal zone"; a desirable place that we'll discuss more in the chapters to follow.

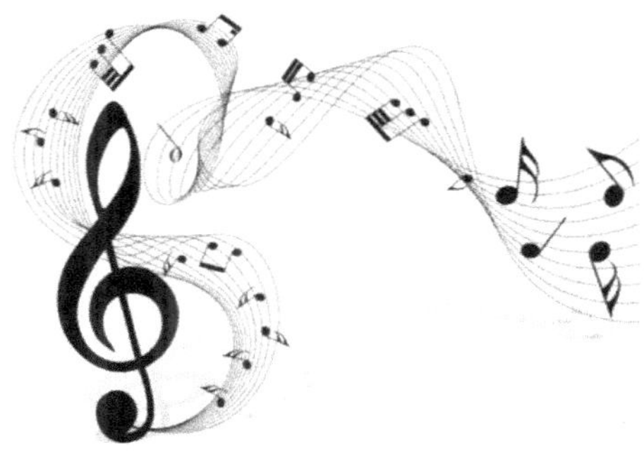

CHAPTER FIVE

Vocal Fusion

In the Zone

When you correctly apply all the internal and external postures we discussed in the prior chapters, and implement them at the right time and place, the magic will start to happen. You are now singing in the "vocal zone".

In the beginning, it's a learning curve, but with due diligence, passion, and the love of singing, it becomes effortless. Being pain-free is the sign that you're singing with a healthy vocal approach and technique. For example, when you warm up, it should feel like your voice just had a nice massage.

Note: When you are no longer experiencing vocal fatigue or pain, it's a clear demarcation that you are making vocal advancement. Therefore, the old saying, "No pain, no gain," does not apply to singing. Once again, this concept corresponds to life. When you're making steady spiritual advancement, the pains of this world are greatly diminished.

The Inner Essence of Your Sound

In order to deliver a captivating performance so the audience/ artist connection occurs, you must tap into the heart of the music you are interpreting. This is the meaning of the expression: "Sing from your heart."

If you want to connect deeper into the heart of the music and lyrics, try reading the lyrics aloud with emotion a few times, as if you were interpreting a theatrical script. Practice this until you can easily access the emotional experience that then translates to the music you're singing. The expression needs to emerge from the core of your soul and become lucid throughout your entire being. This is the optimum mind-set to deliver a non-contrived, emotionally genuine performance.

When you sing, you must pull from past and present emotions or situations. Think of the places you've visited, and the people you've met. You may recall scenes from epic films, as they too can act as a catalyst to help you tap into and deliver a soul stirring performance. When you allow your creative juices to flow using these tools, the artistic expression will convey the song with resonant soulfulness. This will give you not only a greater command of your music, but also a deeper, more profound connection with your audience. As you become a more masterful vocal storyteller, you will be able to transform hearts, captivate minds, inspire souls, and embrace your life's purpose. You can become a vocal global change agent or even a spiritual muse, one who is doing God's work within the world. In the process, you will become a treasured, cherished, and beneficial presence on the planet.

As the human voice is so powerful, it can change the world into an extraordinary place, especially when you infuse divine intention. Your voice can bring about miracles, faith, blessings and hope. Through this process, you will experience a greater sense of inner happiness, purpose, and enthusiasm for life.

Once your voice and life are transformed, once you are filled with the pure love of this transcendental art, your determination and dedication will bring you hours of inner peace, bliss, and contentment. You will be blessed, gifted, and recognized as a unique and precious soul, one who has realized a higher purpose. You will also enjoy the benefits of a richer and more meaningful existence.

Just like a filmmaker or actor, you are transforming your environment into a place of harmony, beauty and happiness by filling it with extraordinary experiences, accessed through divine song and empowering, positive, godly words. These experiences are not only for you. Touching and changing the life and heart of even one person equates to greatness in God's eyes, and leads to a life well lived. *I call it the genius of devotion, for devotion is always rewarded. May we breathe, eat and sleep our higher calling.*

Healthy Vocalizing: Optimum Physical Positions

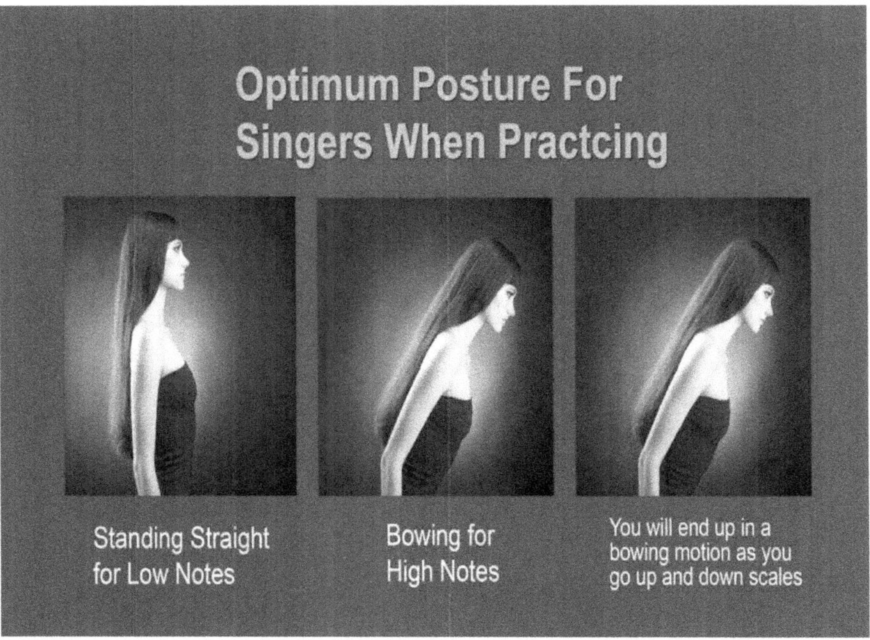

Let's discuss the method of bowing the upper body to obtain further vocal release. Bowing provides tremendous benefits, especially when you're singing into the higher registers. Sound production is normally more difficult in higher registers, such as the middle voice and the head voice. The bowing allows a singer to get up into these registers without causing strain or impairment to the voice, and allows time to build up the needed strength and agility.

Physiologically, muscles that have a tendency to compress in this area will release their hold when the bow is implemented. Therefore, making unwanted muscles release allows a vocalist to build a stronger, more flexible vocal foundation needed for singing in the upper registers. Eventually, when the muscles are strong enough, the need to utilize this bowing posture is retired. However, in many cases, professional singers still incorporate the bowing movement into their performances. An expert performer can incorporate this movement in such a way that it makes it appear as if it were a natural part of their artistic interpretation, while at the same time, saving their voice.

In a more esoteric sense, bowing keeps us humble, helping us accept and embrace life's lessons, as well as changes, with a brave heart. When we start to see these changes as a form of divine purification, then we will understand that they are beneficial for our divine growth. No matter what happens, we know that something good will eventually come out of it, and we can embrace the change, as if it was a stepping stone to the next level of spiritual illumination. As the saints say, the path of least resistance brings about a life free of emotional pain and suffering. As we know, the only resolution is deep meditative communion. Therein is found the strength to endure more difficult times.

Now, let's get back to your voice. Having a solid foundation, and an understanding of healthy singing habits, is crucial. It is very important to warm up your voice correctly before you perform or practice. Just like world-class dancers and Olympic athletes, vocalists have to stretch and warm up their muscles if they want agility, power, and endurance during their performance.

Normally, a minimum of thirty minutes of vocal exercise is the golden ticket to success. However, in order to perfect and master the exercises, one must have a seasoned vocal coach. The coach can give you accurate feedback, while spot-checking your progress. An intuitive coach will guide you with a genuine degree of accuracy, so you can meet your vocal benchmarks and dreams.

It is important to practice the recommended exercises correctly. At the Quantum Vocalist, we make an intelligent assessment of your vocal needs, identify areas you need more support, in and then give you exercises specifically suited for your vocal type and needs. We also incorporate positive educational methodologies. As such, the QV method allows you, the singer or speaker, to advance much faster than with other conventional methods.

When choosing a vocal coach, make sure the person does not take a cookie cutter approach. To do so indicates a lack in his or her natural academic and intuitive talents. If he or she is going to be of real assistance to you, a coach must have the mindset needed to comprehend your individual needs as a vocalist. Choose someone who has a background in positive education, as this method is cutting edge, and can accelerate learning.

Spending even fifteen minutes warming up before a performance, will result in a better sound. It will allow you to have greater command, control, and vocal flexibility.

As we discussed previously, correct singing requires sustaining internal postures in the given moment, and in the precise manner. Therefore, in order to create vocal perfection, intentional sustained muscular postures in the instrument are needed. You can find free videos demonstrating these exercises on the QV website.

Now, since you can't see your vocal apparatus, you must rely on making the unusual sounds described earlier in order to locate and identify the various regions of the voice used in the singing process. As you practice the humble angel or the edgy angel, your successful vocal balance with these two applications will depend on the surrounding muscles staying isolated and relaxed.

Another tip: When you're implementing these sounds, put your hand on your voice box to see whether you're producing the vocal movements correctly, and in a relaxed manner. Remember, if there is too much compression around the larynx muscles, they will become strained. Placing your hand on your voice box will bring your attention to this area, allowing you to relax and release these muscles. This simple process helps you identify subtle variations in the vocal chords and can help you become more acquainted with your instrument.

While your hand is on your voice box, and with your eyes closed, make some sounds, such as "God" or "Om." At the same time, make a mental note, memorizing how your voice box sounds and feels while making these sounds. This exercise will help you understand how to sustain postures and duplicate them at will. Recalling the internal physical sensations of the sounds radiating from your voice box will enhance your awareness of how muscles in the voice box and larynx are affected. Memorizing the physical sensations is the key to mastering the method faster and more efficiently.

Keep in mind that you will need to sustain and implement these positions more rigorously as you go higher into the head voice. This practice will allow you to have greater command over your instrument, so you can produce a more irresistible resonant tone. Since singing higher and louder is more difficult, you will need to implement more of the vocal tools that we discussed previously as you traverse the vocal ranges. Hence, part of the goal is to understand and identify what muscles need to be activated or deactivated throughout the range. In order to help with this process, you must do the exercises. They will help you to have the strength and ability to activate or deactivate them as needed.

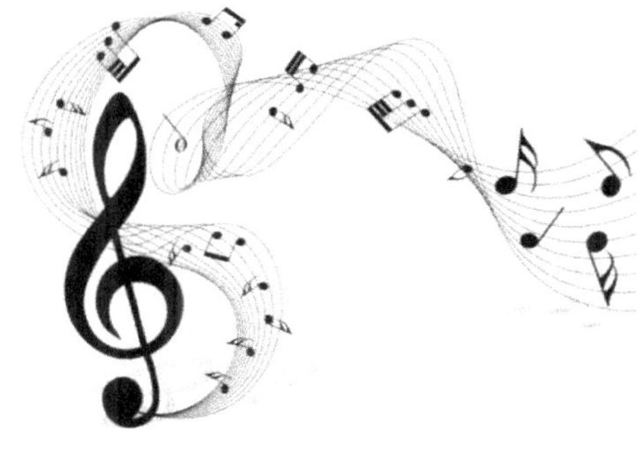

CHAPTER SIX

The Vocal Passages

The Vocal Passages for Women

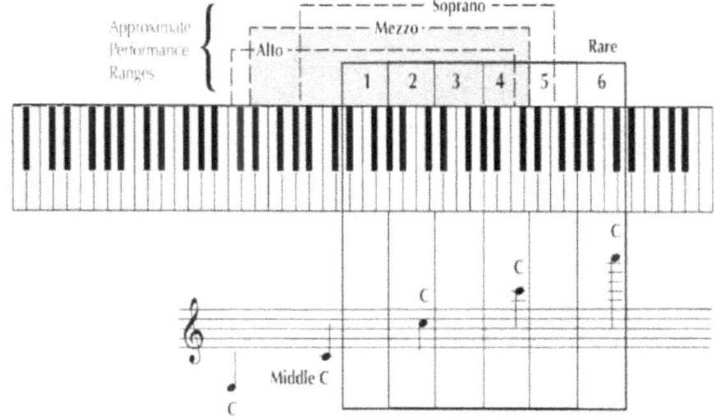

The diagram above shows the vocal ranges for women. Normally, the shift or breaks in the voice occur around the A, A#, B, and Bb, just after the middle C, going up the scale. This occurs again around the D, D#, and E, and it repeats in approximately the same place going up each octave. It will help to familiarize yourself with this chart, and the keyboard, so you understand all of the shifts in the voice. Then, you can be mentally and vocally prepared for them. I like to be prepared for at least two measures ahead of the music. In this way, I can set up the internal postures to navigate the shifts with optimum vocal ease. The above chart will show you which category you fall into as a female vocalist.

Note: being able to sing way above a high C is rare. Only singers like Minnie Ripperton and Mariah Carey have received this God-given gift. These higher notes are also referred to as "whistle tones."

The Vocal Passages for Men

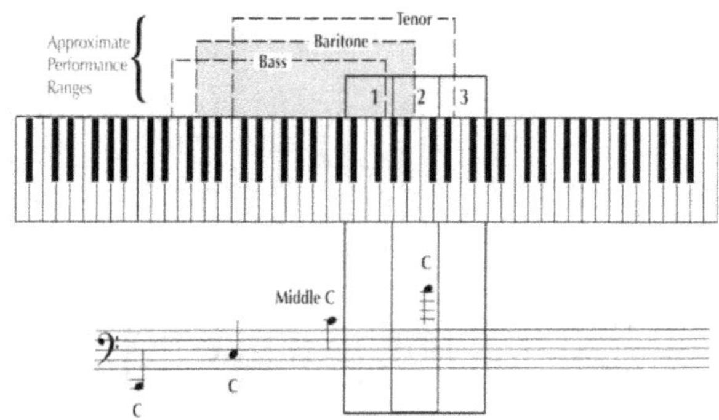

The chart above shows the average voice range for men. It will be advantageous to familiarize yourself with this chart and have a teacher help you identify your range. Knowing your range will help you understand and anticipate where the breaks or shifts will occur. Thinking ahead at least two measures allows you to set up the internal muscular postures to get through these shifts in an effortless and healthy vocal manner. The above chart will show you which category you fall into as a male vocalist.

Your Unique Voice

To develop your unique sound, you must understand how to develop your voice's signature sound. Celine Dion's favorite singers are Barbra Streisand and Whitney Houston. When you listen to Ms. Dion sing, you can hear the influences of these singers in her vocal stylization. That, along with her wonderful French Canadian accent, provides a blend of tones, sounds, shades, and vocal colors. A combination of all these things creates her amazing signature sound.

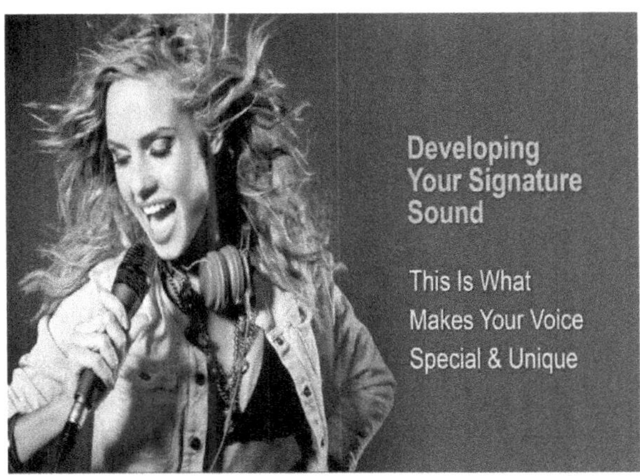

From her example, you too can blend various vocal influences from other singers you admire. By extracting and blending their vocal nuances and infusing them with your own unique flavor, you can create an original, and unique sound.

Less Effort Equals Greater Tonality

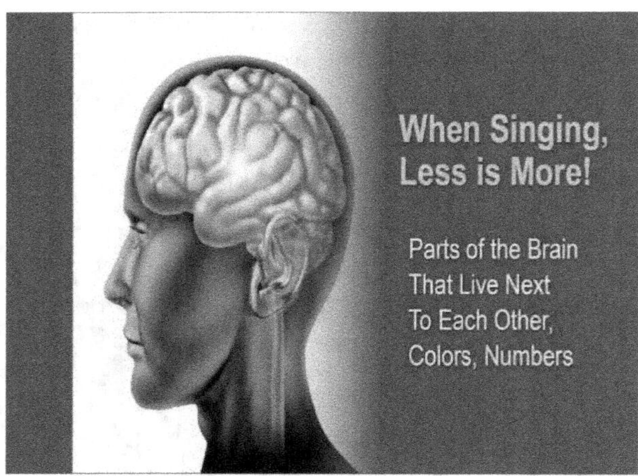

In the above image, we address the theory that less muscular effort requires a freer and more resonant voice. Most singers at times have a tendency to engage too many muscles when they sing. Most singers erroneously use all of the muscles around the voice box, but this practice can wreak vocal havoc. Let's compare this tendency with a neurological discovery made by scientists.

A group of test patients were asked to recite numbers in order to identify what part of their brains were being activated. During the test, a number of the patients commented that they saw the numbers in color. For example, number one was yellow, number four was pink, and number six was green. Scientists observed that the part of the brain that recognizes numbers was located directly adjacent to the part that recognizes colors, so they were actually melding information into one another.

This is what happens to vocalists when they sing and use too many muscles, especially in the higher registers. The muscles used for chewing and swallowing are directly adjacent to the muscles used for singing. Therefore, they are interconnected and have a tendency to interact with one another. Unfortunately, most singers activate the unsuitable muscles, which produces a labored tone and premature vocal fatigue.

Here is another good example: When we were young, we were taught that in order to engage in any physical action, we needed to activate all the tissues, muscles, ligaments and bones in the closest proximity to that action. For example, when you pick up a pen, all the parts associated with this action are engaged—the hand, fingers, and arm, which in turn, activates all of the correlating muscles and ligaments.

However, if singers engage all of the surrounding elements in this way, they end up using too many muscles, which causes the voice to compress and shift in quality. This is apparent during the breaks or shifts in vocal range.

Rule of Thumb:

It's harder to sing higher and louder without a tried and true vocal method giving you the support you need. Thinking a couple of measures ahead of the music allows you to be prepared. Mastering this method is key to ensure your singing success under just about any condition.

The QV method will enable you to get a nice blend, consistent power, and a full resonance in your voice, throughout its entire range. Too much activation can dampen the resounding bell-like tones in the voice. What happens if you put your hand on a bell when you're ringing it? The sound becomes muffled. The same thing happens when you activate too many muscles in the singing process. Doing daily vocal warm-ups while applying vocal corrections will strengthen your voice and build overall stamina. Mastering these internal and external vocal postures will help you obtain the desired grace, ease, and accuracy in singing.

I can't emphasize enough that a singer needs to make constant mental notes, and be attentive, when memorizing the physical sensations. Keying into unusual sounds is necessary to identify, locate, and work the various muscles of your voice. Since the voice is an intangible angelic instrument, you must pay attention to the learning curve. Perfecting each exercise and implementing what you've learned is a top priority in order to create the vocal synthesis. It results in a beautiful, powerful, expressive tone throughout your range. This kind of mastery takes time, due diligence, and dedication. Have faith that your love and passion for your art will see you through. Learn your craft well. In time, this will come when it will become second nature, and then you can sing for the sheer love and freedom of the art.

A Woman's Monthly Moon Cycle

Women are blessed with a monthly moon cycle, a type of sweet purification that can bring life into the world. As singers, we must be aware that the body retains water during this time, which in turn, causes the vocal chords to swell. For this reason, many professional female singers plan ahead and have their music transposed down a whole step or more, in order to ensure that they can deliver a flawless performance during their monthly moon cycle. An entire octave, in many cases, is too much; however, a half a step or more will normally do the trick.

If the symptoms during this time frame are too severe, some vocalists will cancel performances in order to give the needed rest to their bodies. However, we have found that getting acupuncture, combined with Chinese herbs, can help greatly with this kind of discomfort.

Mastering the Microphone

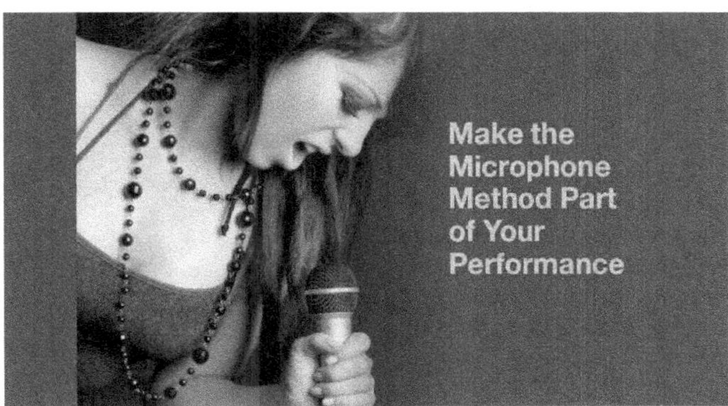

Mastering your microphone can help you reach your head voice with ease. It supports the health and longevity of your voice. When you're singing in the upper registers, your voice may shift in quality or even flip into the next note. That can cause a difficult vocal transition. The image above shows a singer incorporating the bow as part of her artistic expression. Following this example will help you eradicate this obstacle.

When you bow, the muscles around the voice box will release, and allow for an effortless vocal passage into the higher registers. An intelligent singer will bow to save her voice when reaching into those difficult vocal areas. This posture can be incorporated into the emotional deliverance of the song. With practice, a singer can give an authentic, uncontrived, and natural performance, even when incorporating the bow.

The bow is a great analogy for life. I believe it is better to be wrong and happy than right and unhappy. To expound on this idea, there are times when taking the path of least resistance can help you navigate the most difficult situations, or personalities, that you encounter along the way. De-escalation is a word to remember in difficult situations.

Microphone Method: Live & Studio

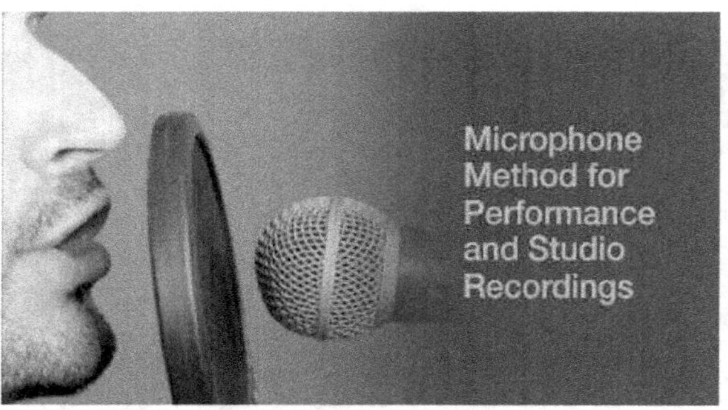

The most effective way to sing into a microphone is called the two-finger microphone technique. This is a simple way to measure proper distance when singing in a medium to soft volume. Take two fingers and put them between you and the microphone. This is the perfect position when you're singing softly or into the mid-decibel ranges. When you're singing words that start with P or B, exaggerate your pout as you position the airflow just slightly over the microphone.

Belting notes is a much more intuitive and calculated process. It is important to interact with your sound person in advance, tuning into the mix coming through your on-stage monitors. A sound check will help you find the exact distance needed to sing into your microphone when belting in the vocal mix or zone. In order to take full advantage of its benefits for your signature sound, it helps to develop an awareness of the microphone positioning. Microphone awareness, combined with a sound check, is essential to create overall ease and comfort in the delivery of your song. It will help you create that mesmerizing magical performance that can stir the souls of your listeners.

When you're moving around, your microphone moves with you as you angle it to pick up your sound efficiently. Singing, while moving your body and head, is a dynamic process. When you're belting your notes, you have to pull the microphone away from your mouth to compensate for the extra volume. This will allow for a fluid and captivating sound design and performance.

Performance, Movement And Sound

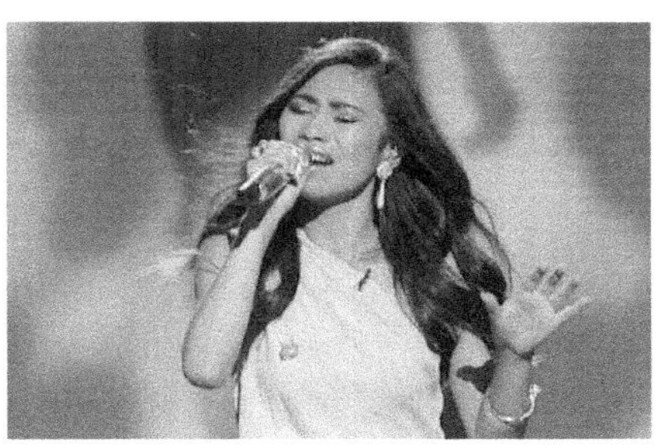

If you have a good sound system, your fallback speakers, also known as stage monitors, will help you gauge what your audience is going to hear. Getting your vocal levels right during the sound check is imperative for delivering an optimum performance. Practice by saying, "God, God, God," into the microphone, with a slight pout at various vocal volumes and distances, to help you dial in the right equalization in the high, low, and mid-ranges of your sound. Make sure you have enough vocal effects, including reverb, delay, and compression, in your overall sound.

Establishing good communication with your sound person ahead of time will allow you to achieve the sound mix and balance you are seeking. It's a good idea to arrange subtle hand signals, incorporated into your performance, to signal your sound person. This will allow you to make seamless changes in your overall sounds and levels during the performance.

This same procedure can be used with your musicians to create a smooth and fluid performance, while maintaining the mood and keeping the audience spellbound.

On another note, when you are getting into difficult vocal areas, a Rule of Thumb is: *When in doubt, just add a little pout.* But don't pout too much or it will distort your sound.

Another Rule of Thumb is:

If you start to feel too much compression around the voice box, add a little bow, and infuse the edgy angel sound with a little yawn, at the correct times. This will get you through the breaks and shifts in your register so you can create an audio and visual masterpiece.

Stay on purpose. Your divine intent can bring about a spiritual awakening in the hearts of your listeners. This will provide a more fulfilling and exuberant performance for you as a vocalist.

Now that you are on your way to mastering these various skills and methods, it's time to prepare for your performance. A great deal of inner preparation is required, so we'll discuss that preparation in the next chapter, especially the most important element—visualizing yourself as a successful singer giving the performance of your life.

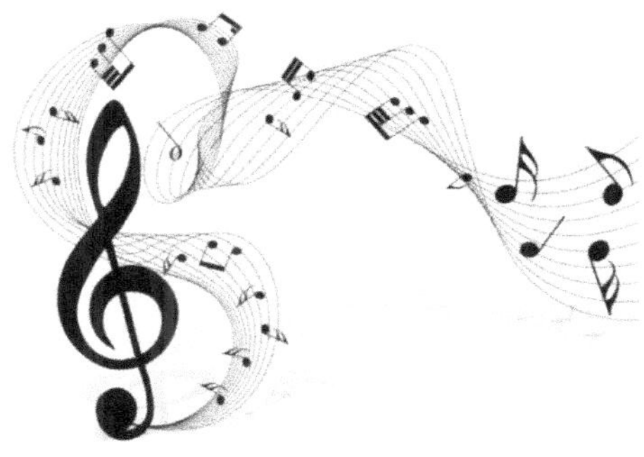

CHAPTER SEVEN

Vocal Confidence

Building Performance Confidence:
Conquering Stage Fright

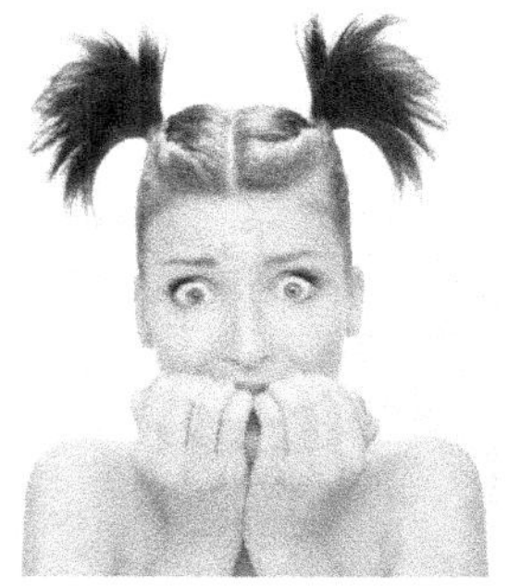

Some vocalists feel uneasy in their stomachs at the very thought of singing in front of an audience. I recommend that vocalists leverage those feelings into their performance and repeat affirmations such as, "I can do this," or "This is easy."

Focus on the things that you like about yourself. Look in the mirror and see yourself as the brilliant, confident, angelic performer you want to be. This will help you push through that wall of fear and emerge with a brave, composed, charismatic, and captivating presence.

Another trick is to overcome stage fright is to gently bounce in place, on the balls of your feet, before you go on stage. This helps shift your mind into a more positive and confident state. Visualization works well. Athletes envision themselves going through the movements in great detail. They mentally work the scenario backwards. They see themselves winning the competition and creating the steps to get there.

Try visualizing yourself, giving the performance of your life, with the audience giving you a standing ovation. You are trying to key into the mood, the mindset, and the inner feelings of this success. This will help you sustain and exude a confident artistic command. This is what I call the performer's euphoria.

Be forgiving of yourself. Every singer either forgets a lyric or misses a note, but a real pro will keep performing, as if nothing happened. The show must go on! Nine times out of ten, the audience won't even notice, unless you bring their attention to it.

Top performers use this visualization process by working the scenario of their performance backwards in their minds. In other words, they visualize the perfect performance, and see the steps needed, in order to achieve that stellar level of confidence.

Visualizing Helps Perfect Your Performance

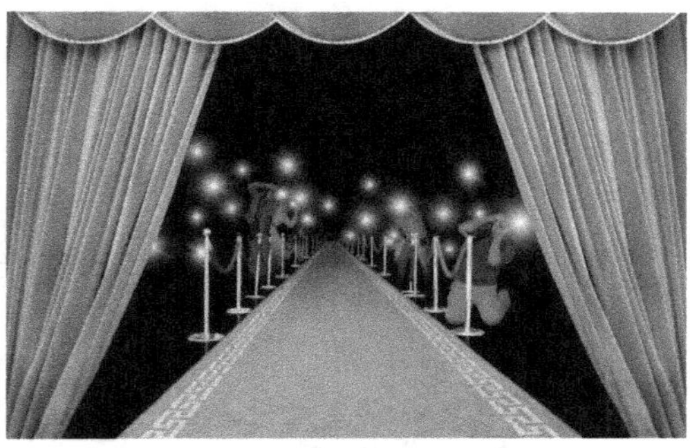

For those of you with performance goals, visualize yourself walking the red carpet at the Grammy Awards, feeling confident, dignified, self-assured, calm, and exuding charisma. Imagine hearing people say, "I absolutely loved your beautiful music. Your angelic performance was mesmerizing and enlightening. Your music saved my life at a time when I needed help the most." Or, "Your singing transformed my heart, and your devotional songs illuminated and healed my soul."

Spend time watching other singers perform in front of a live audience. Absorb the movements and the persona of the singers, especially those whose music and lyrics are positive, uplifting, and inspiring. Inundate your consciousness with the power of positive transformational vibrations can help you experience the best that life has to offer. It can help you live your best life now, moment to moment. Now, close your eyes and imagine yourself being that person, feeling and exuding that unstoppable confidence. Practice these movements in the mirror each day for the fifteen days leading up to your performance.

When the day has arrived and you're ready to step onto the stage, close your eyes and conjure up what you have been observing in the mirror. See yourself brimming with self-assurance, poise, courage, and certainty.

Positive self-talk helps tremendously. Tell yourself that you can do it. Never give up. You can sing wonderfully, with confidence and power, anytime and anywhere. This is because the brain has neuroplasticity, which means, you can retrain your brain at any age. Inner talk and visualization are very effective for empowering and reprogramming the brain. Through this method, you can shift the way you feel about singing and speaking. Putting up Post-it notes around the house, with positive, inspiring affirmations, will get results as well.

Another method for overcoming stage fright is to look slightly past the audience, just over the tops of their heads, toward the back of the concert hall. This will not only relieve your anxiety, but it will also give the audience the illusion that you are connecting with them. Once you regain your emotional equilibrium, you can look at the faces of your audience to create that magical artist/audience connection.

Have you ever felt the exhilarating high that comes from singing spiritual music? Visualize yourself singing for the Divine Creator. See your song as your love offering, a beautiful fragrant flower of gratitude from the heart. In my experience, this faithful gesture takes singing to a whole new level that is off the charts. This inner divine visualization creates the effect of being profoundly, deeply, and mystically awakened on all levels.

It will help if you practice the art of visualization ahead of time. It will combat the fear that you might make a mistake. If you know your material inside and out, you will diminish the fear factor. Make sure you pick an inspiring song that fits your vocal range. Don't be afraid to stretch out a bit and hit a high note every now and again. That helps to captivate and engage your audience.

There is a great saying in the music industry:

To be great, you must breathe, sleep, and eat the music.

But be careful not to overdo it. When you're in the learning curve, and haven't fully mastered the method, the chance for vocal fatigue exists. Always remember to warm up for at least thirty minutes before you perform.

Since your entire body is an intricate part of the vocal instrument, I suggest that in the days leading up to the concert, that you eat a super-food, gluten-free diet for your voice's optimum health. Make sure you don't eat refined sugar or processed foods. The optimum diet is a change of lifestyle where you embrace a super-food, vegetarian, vegan, or raw food diet combination. Drink room temperature water and warm herbal teas such as slippery elm, or room temperature raw organic juices. Don't drink anything a few hours before the performance so you won't need to relieve yourself while you're on stage.

Make sure to warm up and run through your song a few times beforehand. When practicing, remember not to wear out your voice. You must maintain a delicate balance. You want your voice to be warmed up, but also rested, so it's strong enough to carry the entire performance.

For greater inspiration, you can have your favorite devotional picture with you on stage, and say a little prayer, to help center your spirit and connect with your divine purpose as a vocalist and global change agent.

I also suggest incorporating some calming exercises. For example, slow down your breathing and count to ten as you inhale and exhale. When you engage in the above practices, choose a quiet place. Practice contemplative inner prayer or some form of meditation like Bhakti Japa yoga, or Transcendental Meditation, for a minimum of fifteen minutes a day. These mind-calming, inner-centering practices will allow you to access your inner tranquility, and conjure your self-confidence, no matter what is going on around you. These forms of communion have tremendous benefits for your health, including overall well-being, longevity, better mental moods, and they help reduce stress. Try not to be near anyone who may distract you or cause you to become emotionally upset. Did you know that stress, depression, and anxiety actually cause the brain to shrink?

Singing for Crowds of People

The most important thing is to relax and enjoy this amazing opportunity to sing! You are doing what you love to do best, what makes you happiest, and you are fulfilling your divine purpose and your spiritual calling. Put your heart and soul into your performance and it will bring tears of happiness to your audience. There is no high in the world that is as great as making others happy, and inspiring them spiritually. Remember to relax, tune in, and have fun.

When you're performing, if you make a mistake, it's okay. Be forgiving of yourself. Everyone makes mistakes. If you stay calm and forge ahead as if nothing happened, no one will ever notice. Since most people do not have a trained musical ear, they will blissfully enjoy your performance.

Healing Products for Stage Fright

Stage fright can be very debilitating and totally disrupt your performance. The QV website offers a calming tea, and other great products, to help keep you centered, calm, and confident. We can also create a custom-made hypnosis product infused with neuro-linguistic programming (NLP) that works specifically for you and your needs. I find that this works wonders in helping to overcome stage fright or any other dysfunctional habits.

Visit our website: www.theQuantumVocalist.com, and click on the health section, for the list of products or downloadable DVDs. The website is filled with great insights into the health of your body, mind, and soul. You can contact us via email: sing@thequantumvocalist.com.

We also offer products that help with other areas of concern, such as depression, anxiety, weight issues, being happier in life, and having more harmonious relationships. Clients who have followed this advice, and utilized these tools, have successfully overcome stage fright.

Vocal Character: Embody the Song

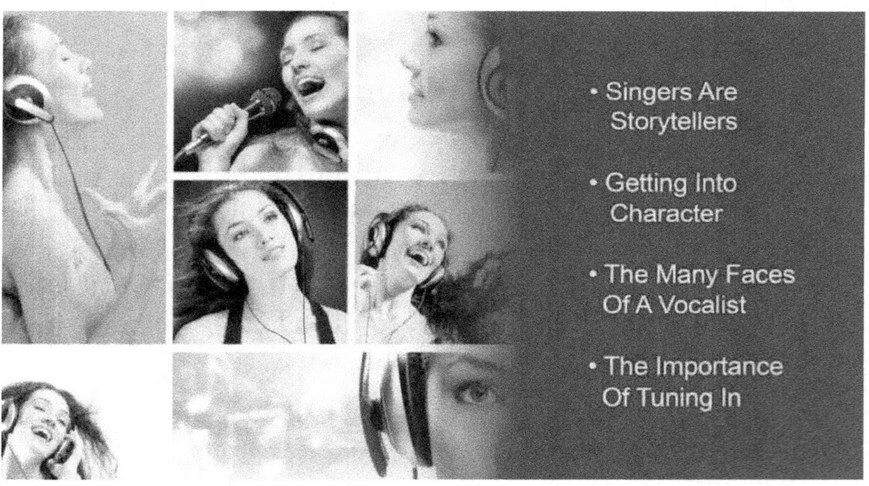

A singer is a lyrical storyteller. Interpreting the music, with a deep emotional connection, enables you to deliver the soul of your song to your audience. It captures their imagination, so they too can take that an inner journey to heaven. It will offer the audience a place they can retreat to, when this world just doesn't make sense. In this way, you will not only enchant the hearts of your audience, but that of God as well. Therefore, tap into your repertoire of emotions, including past and present experiences and especially those that opened your heart to the divine of all. This emotional link is your color palette, your creative canvas. Tapping into it will bring an uncontrived expression across in your song.

In developing an authentic emotional connection with the song and lyrics, it is crucial to sing from the depths of your heart. The heart of your artistic mood, and devotional mindset, will allow the essence of your vocal interpretation to emerge as a memorable, soul-stirring impression.

This vocal formula will awaken a genuine affinity with your audience, providing the cornerstone for greater appreciation of your creative ambience. In essence, this vocal recipe can change lives, and bring audiences to their feet, as you inspire them with your soul-stirring performances.

Coloring Sound: Mastering the Vibrato

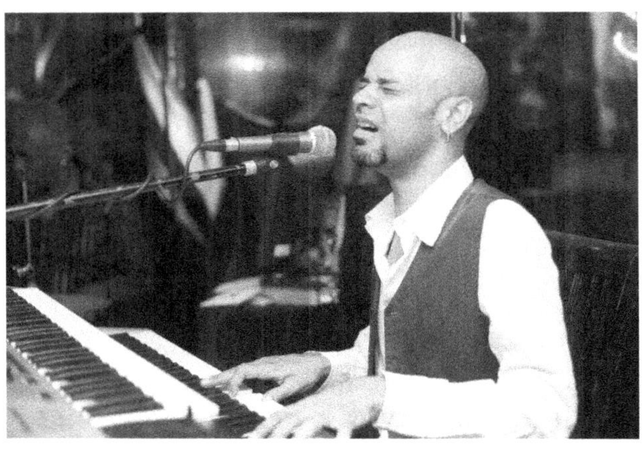

A vibrato adds a brilliant, soulful texture to the overall sound of your voice. In contemporary schools of vocal thought, the popular vibrato is a bit on the fast side. You can measure it in relation to sixteenth notes being played against eighth notes over a 108 tempo. Even in pop, rock, gospel, and forms of devotional music, the vibrato is historically in the faster spectrum. In opera, the norm is to sing the arias with a rapid vibrato as well. The only exception to this rule is the female alto voice, as their vibratos tend to be, in most cases, a bit slower in nature.

You can achieve a steady vibrato in the correct meter in one of two ways:

#1.   Place both hands on your diaphragm, relaxing the muscles as much as possible while pressing inward. Then, release the pressure in a motion, as if you're playing a drum. As you do this, keep your hand stationary on the diaphragm area, while making this drumming movement again, with your hand still on your diaphragm, and delivered in tempo. You may visit QV web site for an example of this technique.

Incorporate this technique, while singing any note that is comfortable to sing, with the word "God" or "Om." The syllable "Om" automatically produces the optimum embouchure. "Om" is a universal sound, representing the divine name of the eternal divinity. The sound helps our hearts connect with our higher spiritual nature, the highest origin of creative inspiration. While doing this, count to five, with your hand still creating the vibrato on your diaphragm. Then, repeat this movement, and count to five without your hands.

Pay close attention to the sound generated by this oscillation process. See how it feels in the voice box, and how it affects the vocal chords, as they open and close. This is an important point in the replication process. Closing your eyes helps to tune into the physical sensation, making it easier to lock in a mental memorization.

#2:   The second method for producing a good, steady vibrato is to put your hands together in front of you, as if you were praying, and shake them in time with the music in a forward and backward motion. The movement should be steady, and the space between the notes needs to be even. Continue to do this in rounds of twenty-five movements, with and without your hands, to get the vocal chords acclimated and adjusted to the internal movements, until the movement becomes spontaneous.

In both instances, it is important to make a mental note of how the exercise feels and sounds. Eventually, you will be able to duplicate it at will, tapping into the vibrato to produce heartfelt, artistic embellishments in your song.

I suggest doing either of these exercises every day for at least five minutes, until the vibrato formulates naturally. When doing these exercises, keep the facial muscles as relaxed as possible.

Vocal Power: Presence and Authority

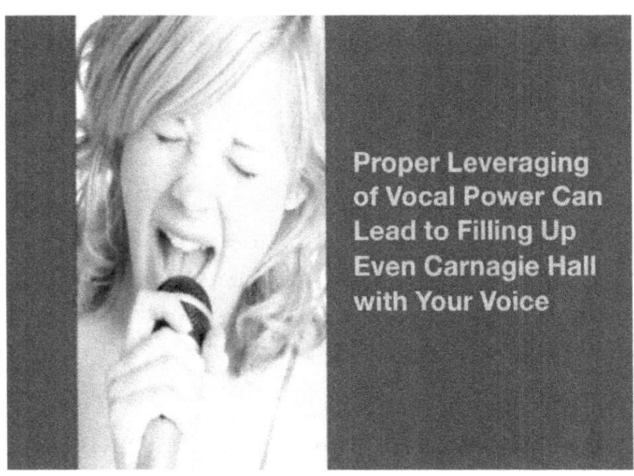

Let's look at the art of belting notes, one of the most dynamic and dramatic aspects of singing. Most singers are eager to achieve the ability to sing loudly. How do great vocal powerhouses belt their notes day in and day out, when they're touring, and doing two shows a night for months on end? They start by getting their voices into the best shape of their lives. This takes committed diligence and perseverance. You have to master the vocal blend, so you don't hurt or fatigue your voice. It's important to remember that yelling is not the same as belting your notes in the blend, because yelling pulls the internal lower vocal muscles up. This is also known as pulling the chest. In addition, yelling will cause tremendous vocal stress on the voice.

Mastering the vocal blend will give you the ability to belt your notes in a way that allows you to leverage an expansive amount of vocal power. With this in mind, when you blend it with the QV method, you will learn to sing with absolute vocal power, as you correctly deliver vocal excellence. Then, you can belt in the blend for hours and days on end, without having to shout.

Shouting will cause vocal fatigue and can eventually lead to vocal damage. Vocal damage occurs when you are not careful with your vocal delivery, and have not had good guidance in developing strength, flexibility, and agility in your approach to the vocal apparatus.

The QV method offers the tools a vocalist needs to get through even the most demanding vocal situations, including concerts, tours, or long hours in the recording studio.

The Benefits of Intuitive Listening

For a singer, intuitive listening is just as important as singing. In the listening process, a singer will first tune into the song to learn the form of music. Once that is established, the singer can focus on perfecting the artistic interpretation, while still delivering a healthy, heartfelt production of the inner mood and meaning of the lyrics and melody.

Remember to anticipate the upcoming passages and be prepared. For example, if the passage calls for you to sustain long tones, you will need to prepare by taking in twice the amount of air. Having the foresight to know when to implement the various vocal modalities, at a precise moment, will help you achieve an almost seamless and effortless performance. If you are facing complex vocal embellishments, with the vibrato sung up into the head voice while belting, you must first set up your internal vocal posture. You will need to navigate and manipulate the muscles with enough agility, strength, and flexibility to get through the most complex and challenging vocal passages, thus allowing you to receive greater creative inspiration.

In the intuitive listening process, you can gain vocal inspiration by listening to music from your favorite devotional artists, watching meaningful music videos, or attending inspiring live concerts. When you filter this through your own creative lens, it can give rise to a wonderful, new, and original transcendental masterpiece. It is always important to immerse yourself in the kind of music that encourages a favorable devotional life experience.

The Singer's Dance:
Creating Captivating Performances

Did you know that fifty percent of what an audience responds to is visual? By mastering the art of the Singer's Dance, and incorporating it into your performance, you will create a visual ambiance that is enthralling, captivating, and mesmerizing for you and your audience.

The Singer's Dance is a blend of acting, miming, and dancing, and can create a visual tapestry that will capture the imagination, attention, and hearts of your listeners. The entire persona of the singer, with all elements working in concert together, brings forth the visual components that enliven your audience. The Singer's Dance will help you learn to interpret your song, in an authentic manner, as you project a radiant and confident persona.

It can be helpful to observe other singers, and mimic their movements, facial expressions, and hand gestures. Spot-check yourself in a full-length mirror, or with the help of a caring, encouraging friend or family member, who will help you evaluate your movements in conjunction with your singing. Daily practice will help you achieve optimum results. When you feel comfortable, you can infuse your own flavor of creative interpretation into the movements. In this way, you can create your signature presentation. The goal is to achieve a natural and fluid integration of the movements that supports the song's inner divine intent.

In order to key into the mood and emotional character of your song, visualize yourself being the singer that you observed. The benefit of a vocal and performance coach is that he or she can effectively assist you with your choreography. The coach will spot-check your movements with expert guidance, accuracy, and feedback. A vocal artist, whether on-site or on-line, is a transcendental storyteller. A successful performance occurs when the fusion of singing, acting, dancing, and the higher divine intention all harmonize.

Higher intention is the desire to be a gift to your audience. You want to send out positive, inspiring, prayerful vibrations, while you show them a portal of time that can be life-transforming. You want to bring them renewed feelings of faith, courage, hope, and comfort.

Choose songs that give people insights and wisdom about life. Such songs will, in turn, bring the riches of the world to your feet. I believe that the most priceless gem of this planet is a selfless, loving compassion for all beings. In God's eyes you are highly prized, if you touch and uplift even one person. From one person, you can go on to touch the hearts of thousands or even millions of people. When it all comes together, this synthesis has the power and grace to ignite, bless, and stir the souls and hearts of your audience with flames of Divine light.

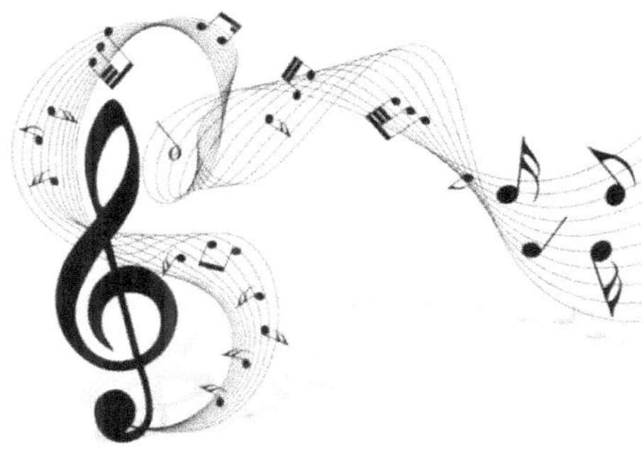

CHAPTER EIGHT

Vocal Visualization

Success as a Transformational Artist

Perhaps you've heard about the power of intention, and visualizing in your dreams, from people like Oprah, the late Wayne Dyer, or from progressive Christians like Joel Olsteen. This concept actually dates back to ancient religious scriptures, and is still very relevant today. Visualization can be applied to singing, and when infused with dedication, commitment, faith, and focus, you can achieve a level of elite world-class brilliance, creative expression, and inspiration.

Here is an example: Imagine walking down the red carpet as a seasoned, award-winning artist, comfortable and confident in yourself. Even if you're content with your vocal achievements, or spiritually satisfied and enriched in your purpose, visualization can help you go deeper into the mindset of the interpretive transformational performance arts. Keeping your heart filled with gratitude will take you to that endless world of eternal happiness. The highest use of your voice is to inspire hearts to seek that place of eternal grace.

Take a moment before you practice, or perform, to tune in to the higher source, and ask for Divine creative inspiration and guidance. See yourself as a spiritual muse, meant to inspire all to have open hearts that embrace the highest absolute reality. This helps keep the stream of creativity flowing into your soul.

The QV Formula in Review

Let's recap what we have discussed so far. Singing is all about mastering the vocal intention. We are working to blend and infuse that which will offer us the agility and strength to direct, balance, and activate the correct singing muscles. When the QV method is applied correctly, it allows you to create a powerful vocal presence, in any style of music. We are looking for a seamless, internal vocal orchestration that will, over time, take your singing, and your life, to its highest and best possible result, far beyond your highest expectations.

Good Singers are Worth Their Weight in Gold

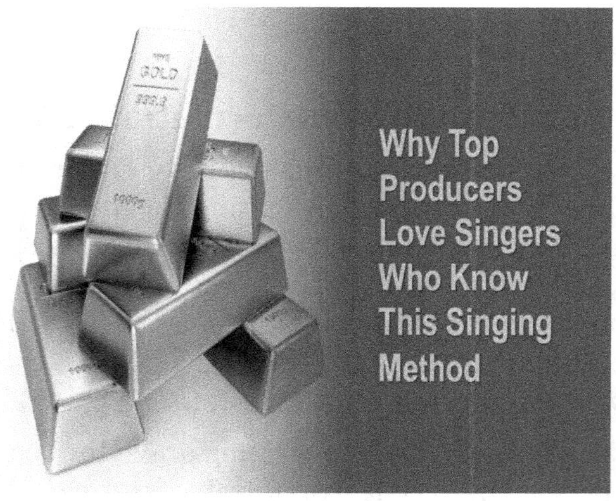

Mastering the Quantum Vocalist singing method can help an aspiring vocalist, or an already established performing artist, to be in great demand with music producers. As the saying goes, you will be "Worth your Weight in Gold". A vocal curriculum of this caliber will ultimately help you achieve and command greater attention, vocal status, and value in the spiritual, and secular, entertainment industry.

When you master the QV method, you will be able to perform continuously, with no vocal downtime, and with a deep, soulful inner resonance. Regardless of whether you are performing devotional, inspiring, or mainstream music, producers will take notice.

On a more esoteric level, I see vocalists as messengers of God. Our message should be one of lyrical encouragement, inspiration, and enlivenment. It should help heal hearts, mend broken minds, and give lasting happiness to others. I encourage singers to help inspire the souls of this world, and to find bliss in musical magic. Allow your listeners to embrace a dreamlike land that is filled with the most astonishing delight. Your voice can be the gift of a great benediction that feels like the "happily ever after" we all seek. Over time, this gift will flourish, offering inner strength, and the stamina, needed to transcend life's most difficult times.

I see a singer's purpose as being a beneficial presence in the world that can gratify the soul and feed our need for creative contentment. We want to encourage hearts so they open up to the heavenly call of Divine love, to be a benevolent, valuable, and precious change agent on the planet. When we become a blessing to all, through our singing or speaking, we become God's golden-hearted angels and we are worth more than our weight in gold.

Vocal Styles and Embellishments: Sound Textures, Shades and Colors

Vocal styles are made up of various vocal tones, colors, shades, textures, and embellishments, along with phrasing and timing. Understanding this can help build and expand upon your own unique angelic signature sound. It all depends on how a particular genre of music is approached and constructed. It makes sense, for example, that singing opera as opposed to contemporary country, pop, rock, gospel, or devotional styles of music, necessitates the use of different sets of vocal variations. The intricate internal vocal navigation comes into play in a different way, including lyrical articulation. This drives the correct formula for optimum resonance production.

When all of these components come together under the right vocal condition, a wonderful embellishment is created. Some embellishments may use the same vocal combinations, and internal muscular flexibility, as faster or slower applications.

Here are a few examples:

Spiritual gospel, R&B, and most contemporary secular and devotional forms of music, use a speaking posture within the vocal apparatus. On the other hand, classical opera has a floaty, heady sound, with an almost constant vibrato, wafting through the notes. You need to stay mindful of the style of music you are singing, and what parts of your singing mechanism you need, to activate or isolate.

Originally, musical theater had a very edgy, or crying angel sound. This sound was primarily produced in the speaking voice. You can hear this when you listen to musical theater greats, such as Ethel Merman, who is celebrated as "the first lady of musical theater." Today, however, singers in the musical theater genre use a cleaner, more legit sound, fused with pop, and at times, an operatic texture.

To clarify, a legit sound is a trained voice that was, at one time, essential on Broadway. This vocal approach provided a clear, defined shaping of the lyrics, in essence, a type of Broadway *Bel Canto*. Today, it is blended with other vocal styles and modalities that have shaped modern musical theater.

Vocal genres such as gospel, contemporary devotional forms of music, pop, R&B, folk, and rock, use more of the speaking voice, with a medium to fast vibrato. While incorporating the edgy angel, and the humble angel inflections, at optimum times, each style is formulated to convey and achieve a particular mood, color, texture, and shade. The phrasing of the music will reflect the specific characteristics of the particular temperament of the music. The correlating muscular activation, and isolation, must be applied in order to deliver the artistic expression that each style demands. Grasping and mastering these tonal differences will give you greater insight and a more variegated vocal palette from which to choose.

Being Vocally Prepared

Being a prepared singer will help you create magical, musical experiences. To get the most out of the QV method, you need to record yourself, so you can become familiar with the resonant sound of your voice. When you learn to critique what you do and do not like, it allows for greater mastery in your artistic design and performance. It also opens your sound up to creating unique and fresh embellishments.

A singer must always be prepared for what's coming next. You need to anticipate changes, so you can set up the internal vocal postures accordingly. This is a form of vocal liberation, because it frees up the voice for lasting, fluid musical transition, a metaphor that can translate into leading a well-orchestrated life. It will offer you emancipation of the soul from the mundane, materialistic existence. You can become a master at transforming life's tribulations by singing, chanting, or speaking prayerful, positive, spiritual words, not only to yourself externally and internally, but to others as well. The effects are simply astounding, and can help you achieve a great life, on all levels.

Words are powerful. Choose them well so they can turn your life into a living heaven. When your words are filled with inspiring, positive beliefs, intonations, and visualization, you can speak or sing your way to a brighter day. This is what I call "applied soul intelligence," a philosophy that can help change the world.

The Origin of Modern Music: Spiritual Gospel Music

The foundation of modern music can be traced back to the start of American Spirituals, also known as gospel music. Much of our modern music has been profoundly influenced through the origin of the African American religious experience, as far back as the early seventeenth century. This form of music was used to provide solace, hope, and a sense of communion with God among subjugated Africans. This early religious music marked one of the historical cornerstones that brought forth a nation founded on Godly principles, and ushered in an anointed and illustrious start to America.

Such a tradition was steeped in Godly temperament, one that encourages singers to intuitively feel the music coming from a higher source before singing it. Pop, R&B, jazz, blues, folk, musical theater, rap, and some contemporary country music, have all been influenced by gospel music. Gospel singers take no breaks as they traverse all three voices in their range, while belting notes with power, command, and riveting emotion.

This spiritually based vocal method of gospel music is one of the fundamental keys of the QV method, because it allows the singer to maintain a fusion of power, command, and soulfulness. In many cases, there is no vocal downtime when gospel singing is combined with a cutting-edge method like QV.

If you analyze some of the world's most prestigious vocal methods, you'll see that they are an amalgamation infused with gospel components, a primary foundation of modern American music. This is our heritage. Other components of leading vocal methods come from the eighteenth century *Bel Canto*. Therefore, the QV method is imbued with the world's most elite vocal techniques, paired with our own intuitive, creative, and analytical discoveries.

Let's take a moment to examine gospel vocal methodology. Sounds like the edgy angel, the yawn, and the humble angel, are unorthodox in nature, and can be traced to a particular set of emotions and techniques utilized and in gospel singing and *Bel Canto*.

Bel Canto is a vocal method that flourished in the eighteenth and nineteenth centuries. It was popularized in the music of Handle, Mozart, and Rossini. Operas have always demonstrated the most dramatic use of the technique. The sounds of the edgy and crying angels create an emotionally gripping color in a vocalist's palette of music, core elements for keeping the voice fit and healthy. They produce a consistent, and vibrant, resonant tonal quality. These offer a vocal strength, durability, flexibility, power, and connectedness that will result in executing highly florid passages, within all three voices.

These tones transform sound into a rich and artistic masterpiece. For instance, the edgy angel sound relates to the emotion of crying, which emerged when enslaved African Americans were experiencing deep tribulations. They transformed their tears and fears into soul-stirring sounds for God. The edgy angel pulls the vocal chords together in a zipping motion, and allows the singer an effortless delivery, throughout their entire range.

When combined with other internal postures, the magical effect of effortless singing results in absolute purity of expression. The humble angel sound, also from African American roots, sounds like "ugh." When we can't control our external environment, we can control the inner landscape of our souls' experiences, through consistent inner and outer inspirational dialogue, infused with visual and audio affirmations. A person who conquers the mind also conquers the world, and is always a winner!

The humble angel pushes down on the upper larynx muscles, creating the needed room to get over the soft palate area, allowing the singer to connect and blend into the head voice. When you combine the two sounds of the humble and edgy angels, you can soar effortlessly into any of the three voices.

Since gospel music emerged during the days of slavery, we can view it as a miraculous metamorphosis, in which the madness was transformed, into musical, spiritual masterpieces. Through their mammoth struggles, African slaves found music to be a holy portal leading to Heaven's door, a space of inner solace, and an eternal place in God's heart. While they were not able to escape their physical situations, they achieved spiritual freedom through singing spiritual songs. They literally transposed their pain and suffering into something divinely empowering, turning the situation into a divine legacy.

We can apply this to our lives as we transcend daily woes, anxieties, pains, suffering, stresses, and depression. We can turn our hearts to the world of spiritual, cosmic, sonic vibrations through our holy songs, sounds, and chants. Why not take this opportunity to step into the portal of divine happiness, not only in this life, but the next as well. I see divine music as an eternal spiritual spa for the soul, where you can become your own best friend, spiritual guide, and hero, as you follow in the footsteps of the anointed saints and sages.

Spiritual singing can be your gateway to the fountain of youth and radiant emotional rejuvenation. It allows you to take an emotional and mental vacation into a sublime, kind, and ever-forgiving heavenly place. Know that this paradisiacal place is there for you, on demand, anytime and anywhere. With this powerful tool, you can break down even the highest or hardest of emotional walls, through your music and your prayers. All you need to do is tune into your own inspiring, devotional song or chant. A simple hum, or saying the syllable "Om", or the word "God", over and over again, can bring great relief to a heart that needs healing. When you're in pain of any kind, this formula of divine song, blended with hypnotherapy and NLP, works miracles. Visit our website to learn more. www.TheQuantumVocalist.com.

Creating Vocal Magic: Divine Sound Design

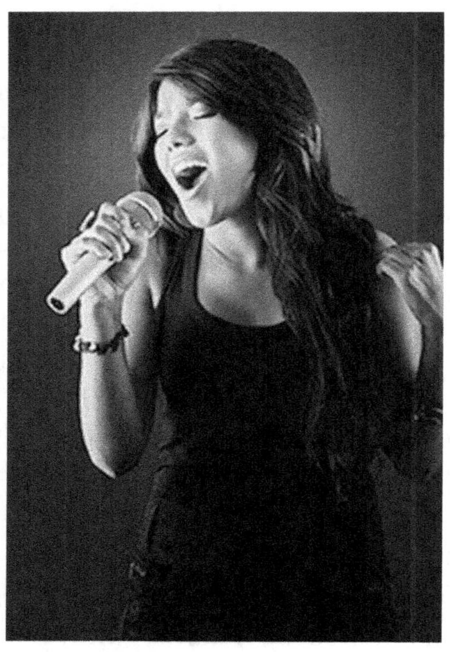

Once you master the more technical aspects of music, it will become second nature, like riding a bike. Once that occurs, you can forget most the theory and scientific methodology, and just connect with your own intuitive, inspired, improvisational creative singing. In this way, your creative signature, expression, interpretation, and sound design, will emerge. You will have the freedom to interpret the music through your own natural creative filter and sensibility, sanctioning your sense of instinctive flair with tasty, improvisational colorization.

The Science of Vocal Fitness:
A Healthy Body Equals a Robust Voice

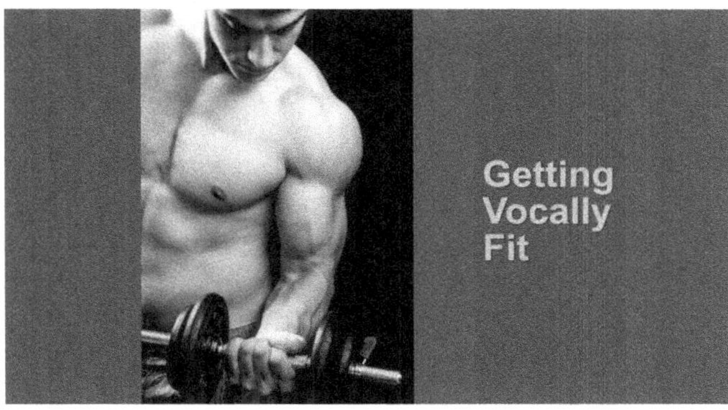

Your body is your instrument. A healthy body equals a captivating, resonant voice. For a professional singer, learning how to keep it at the gold standard of vocal fitness is essential. Part of this process is making sure you keep up with all the vocal exercises that the QV method prescribes. You can find some examples of exercises, for free, on our website: www.TheQuantumVocalist.com.

This is the way to achieve a world-class standard of singing, and obtain the vocal stamina needed, to protect your vocal muscles from atrophy. Therefore, if you want to be great, you will need to go into a rigorous training program to fly high. If you study with attentive astuteness, and complete dedication, you can circumvent the normal 10,000-hour benchmark previously set to master any art, and obtain greatness within 200 hours of intensive attentive study.

Therefore, if you want to fly high in the spiritual and secular music worlds, you must to put in the time. If you want to sing just for the fun of it, practice at least three times a week, for a minimum of 30 minutes.

The Quantum Vocalist also has a set of exercises that address those with the busy lifestyle who needs a regimen that can be done anywhere at any time. To purchase this product, called "QV Quick Warm Ups Anytime Anywhere," send an email to: sing@TheQuantumVocalist.com; or visit: www.TheQuantumVocalist.com, for free vocal tips that show these warm-ups as our gift to you.

To recap, vocal exercises are heavy lifting for the voice, because they build vocal range, muscle tone, strength, agility, power, and flexibility. When you engage in vocal exercises, you tangibly build the solid foundation needed to achieve great singing. When you get your muscles in shape, you'll be able to sing with greater ease, command, and coordination. Again, for casual singers, I suggest practicing from thirty to sixty minutes. For professionals or aspiring professionals, it should be two to four hours a day. Remember, the voice is a delicate instrument. You can't go to the music store and purchase another set of vocal chords. You have to learn how to take good care of the ones you have. Tune in when the voice feels tired, and give it a rest.

Sing Great, Conquer Bad Habits

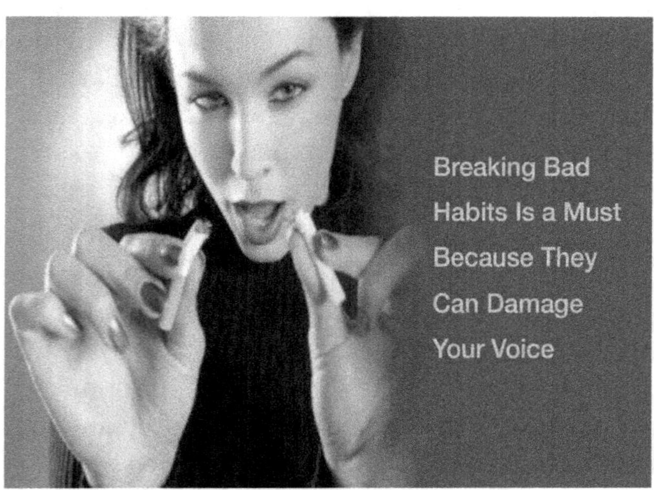

Let's talk about the importance of breaking bad habits that can deteriorate the beauty and power of your voice, body, and soul. Eliminating them as soon as possible is vitally important. You must adopt a lifelong regime of good habits, so brain training is essential. Smoking cigarettes, drinking alcohol, drug abuse, junk food, refined sugar, deep-fried foods, fat-laden commercial dairy, and red meat can all be a source of irritation to the vocal apparatus, and they cause inflammation in the body.

The better you take care of your body, the better you will sing and your emotional health will improve as well. I advocate a super-food and healthy vegan—vegetarian diet. Avoiding red meat altogether is a good thing, because it can often be hard to digest, causing acid reflux. In this scenario, the acid from the stomach can travel up the trachea/windpipe and burn the vocal chords, causing permanent, irreversible damage.

If you study the anatomy of the human digestive system, you'll notice it resembles an herbivore's digestive system, such as those of cows, bunnies, and horses. It does not resemble the carnivore's digestive system. If you embrace a vegetarian, plant-based diet, you'll sing and look better, as you achieve overall wellbeing, health, happiness, and longevity.

Your body should run like a custom Lamborghini, an elite machine in which you would only use the finest octane fuels. Putting only organic super-foods into your multi-million dollar instrument (your body) will keep your priceless, divine, vocal equipment in stellar condition, similar to the analogy of a world-class automobile. Also, don't forget to exercise. I highly recommend devotional dance as it parlays into your performance. You can visit our web site to see some of these various forms of dance movements: www.TheQuantumVocalist.com.

In all, your body is a sacred instrument for creating enlightening experiences here in this world. It is your most precious and treasured possession, and it needs to be properly tuned and cared for. In the same vein, you need to stay mentally fit. Activities like meditation, prayer, and mantra chanting, can train the mind to remain calm and centered, allowing you to adapt quickly and easily to any situation. You can train the mind to detach, tune-in, and block out all distractions. As they say, God's show must go on!

The use of visualizations, neuro-lingusitic programming, (NLP), and hypnotherapy can help correct bad habits. Visit our website to find some helpful hints on how to address bad habits.

Go to www.TheQuantumVocalist.com and order our CD: "Conquering Bad Habits." This CD incorporates NLP and hypnotherapy, and is created from a certified Quantum University practitioner.

QV can also customize a program specifically to your needs that will help with addictions and undesirable habits, including food, smoking, drinking, drugs, stress, anger, low self-esteem, ideal weight, getting fit not fat, and dealing with depression.

The Formula for Vocal Endurance: Vocal Warm-Ups and Practicing

Have you ever heard your voice on someone's answering machine? Were you amazed by the way you sounded? What you hear internally is different from what the external world hears. The sounds you hear have gone through the layers of your cranium. Recording your practices is essential to memorizing your overall tone, and how it sounds, to the external world. In this way, you can make the needed adjustments.

If you don't have a recording device handy, you can stand a foot away from a wall and sing into it, funneling your sound into a small spot. The sound will reflect your voice back to you, giving you an opportunity to hear it in real time. That way, you will be able to critique your voice, and make the needed corrections, with a higher degree of accuracy. Simply put, memorizing your resonant tone will help you master your lyrical verbalization. Don't forget, listening to music in your favorite genre, is just as important as singing, because it is part of ear training. This attentive, in-depth studying supports your ability to comprehend timing, articulation, phrasing, and vocal embellishments.

However, one must be careful. Repetitive listening can be like brain washing, or mind reprogramming. Focus on spiritually uplifting devotional music that gives rise to a beautiful mental temperament and inner contentment. To have your best life now, it is best to engage and inundate your senses in transformational, empowering, positive divine arts, media, and entertainment.

Vocal Calibration: Singing in Tune

For some people, singing in tune can be difficult, especially if you didn't learn it at an early age. Start by closing your eyes and trying not to over-think the sound of the note. Try to feel the sound in your body as an emotional vibration, and not as a mental process. If you practice diligently, regularly, and with proper guidance, then this procedure will normally do the trick in balancing the note.

A vocal tuner can show you, on a visual gauge, when your note is in tune. Play a note on the piano, then sing the note, and see how close you are getting with the tuner. Adjust your sound accordingly. You have to be patient, and diligent, to master this process. It might take a little longer without an on-site vocal coach, but it is possible to do on your own. You can order a vocal tuner on our website at: www.TheQuantumVocalist.com.

Once you've balanced the harmonic resonant sound of the note, including memorizing the physical sensation, you will have successfully mastered the intonation and vocal tuning process. You must be patient; however, since this process takes years to master. Try engaging in either of these two exercises every day, for at least thirty minutes. To avoid getting "pitchy," you can apply steady tension on your diaphragm muscle, when the tension vacillating on your diaphragm causes the note to go out of tune.

Now that we've explored visual and physical techniques to improve your voice, let's look at some lesser known methods that will allow your voice to bring out its unique essence and tone. This is what will set you apart from other singers.

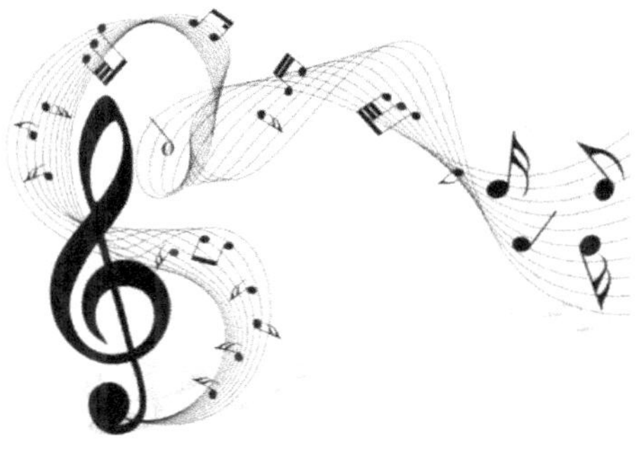

CHAPTER NINE

Nurturing Your Voice

Caring for Your Sacred Instrument

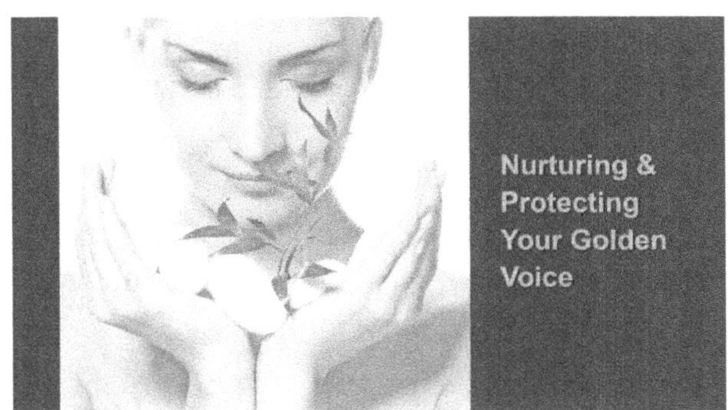

The voice needs to be carefully cultivated, cared for, and nurtured since it is a very delicate instrument. I suggest using a vocal atomizer with a drop of essential organic oil, such as lavender, mint, eucalyptus, or licorice, before your performances. Adding the use of the vocal atomizer to your thirty-minute warm-up before a performance will keep the vocal muscles pliable and resilient. You can find essential oils on our website.

Your voice allows you to bring forth something unique and beautiful, making the world a much better place. You can create a magical atmospheric Utopia for your listeners. Through the use of your soulful sound, you have the power to transform the mundane world into an enchanting and fascinating place. Your voice, body, mind, and soul need to be loved, guarded, and looked after with mindfulness. Being passionate about your art makes it an exciting and fun journey.

If you find it difficult to embrace a healthy lifestyle and break bad habits, I encourage you again to listen to a recording called "Conquering Bad Habits." We can also create a custom recording for you to address your specific needs.

Email: sing@TheQuantumVocalist.com for more information, or visit our web site at www.TheQuantumVocalist.com.

We will help you train and reprogram your mind, and transform undesirable habits, by developing new and beneficial ones. Always remember that your voice allows you to bring forth something unique and beautiful, making the world a much better place. This makes you a remarkable soul.

The Singer's Diet: Healing Super-Foods

It's a good idea not to eat for at least two hours before a performance. When you eat, your energy is redirected from the body and mind to focus on the digestive process. Therefore, the mental process is delayed, which in turn, will slow your reactionary time, creating a labored delivery of your vocal performance.

Try eating light foods like organic veggie juices, healthy healing salads, soups, and steamed veggies, at least four hours beforehand. Drink only purified water, herbal tea, or fresh organic juices, two hours before your performance. Since the body is an intrinsic part of your vocal instrument, the better you take care of it, the better you'll feel and the better you'll sing. Again, remember that vocalists who eat red meat run the risk of developing heartburn and acid reflux, which can burn vocal chords and cause permanent damage. After this happens, some singers never regain their ability to perform at maximum capacity, and others permanently lose the use of their head voice. This is a serious health risk for singers. If you are deeply passionate about singing, you'll do whatever it takes to maintain a healthy lifestyle.

When your body is ill, try to use natural remedies, though allopathic medicine has its place, naturopathic is our first choice. You can find more information about alternative natural cures online, and learn how to replace sugar with healthy substitutes, such as xylitol, stevia, and coconut sugar. These sweeteners have a low glycemic level that is important for overall health. For those who are watching their weight, they are also low in carbs.

It is best to choose only the finest organic oils like flax, sesame, coconut, and olive oil. Ghee, which is clarified butter, can be used if you need a little dairy. Try to make everything you eat organic.

Note: Olive and flax oils should only be ingested cold and never heated.

Balanced proteins, such as beans, nuts, and seeds, give you a complete, lean, clean super protein. Super-foods, including all organic fruits and veggies, as well as herbs, supply quality nutrition without harmful pesticides. Items such as chia seeds, flax seeds, and hemps nuts are packed with Omega-3s. There are other great super-foods, such as spirulina, nutritional yeast, quinoa, and brown rice, that are also a good addition to your diet. These high quality foods provide tons of antioxidants and are nutrition-rich.

Personally, I like to take enzymes with meals. I recommend this to anyone over fifty years of age. Visit our website, and click on the Health Products page, to learn more about super-foods, get some recipes, and learn about healing products: www.TheQuantumVocalist.com.

In addition, adding daily prayer or meditation, yoga, tai chi, deep breathing, visualization, and positive affirmations, are extraordinarily beneficial. When things don't go the way you want them to, positive affirmations allow you to transcend the most challenging of situations and come out on top, always the winner.

I once read that forgiving, or as we say in our Hawaiian culture, "Ho'oponono," is a brilliant idea for the preservation of one's happiness. Holding a grudge, or sending unkind vibrations to someone else, is like drinking poison and expecting the other person to die. An intelligent person will choose the higher positive road, a more harmonic alignment, and a much happier alternate reality.

Humming and singing positive spiritual songs during the day will also help you on your road to happiness. This is one of the best ways to manage stress. Stress ages the body and lowers the immune system, opening the door to disease. Anger, irritation, frustration, and depression cause the brain to shrink like a prune—not a fun prognosis. Whatever you're going through, remember to think spiritual happy thoughts, as it will keep you flying high.

Daily exercise is also essential. I recommend positive meditative or divine dance as a great form of exercise, and it can be incorporated into your performance movements. Many of these life-enriching methods are modalities you can find on my website. Devotional music, higher spiritual thoughts, uplifting beneficial affirmations, and empowering words are the recipe for a sensational life, filled with balance and bliss.

An Angelic Gift

The following story is my personal testimony around a divine visitation of sacred inspiration. A few years ago, I was going through some devastating business dealings that were affecting both my personal and social life. At that time, I was diagnosed with lupus, compounded with a severe gall bladder infection, a major setback in both my life and my career. I was so ill, I ended up in the emergency room where the doctors told me I'd be lucky if I made it through the night. They said I needed to have emergency surgery in order to survive. Apparently, my white blood cell count was off the charts, and they wouldn't release me until I promised to have the surgery.

I agreed, and the next thing I knew, I was on my way to the main hospital and yet another emergency room. That was when I started hearing angelic voices that were speaking in the sweetest and most loving way, telling me that this seemingly life-saving emergency surgery was not needed. They promised to take care of me, and I knew on a visceral level that I was being divinely protected through their immaculate mercy.

I had not considered myself a devout person at that time. I hadn't done any real spiritual work, or been that much of beneficial presence on the planet, as of yet. However, since the angelic voices were so sweetly persistent about my not having the surgery, I decided to follow their advice. I took a leap of faith, and from a visceral place, informed the doctors that I would be declining the surgery. The doctors were so emphatic that I had to have it, that it took a bit of wrangling in order to get them to agree to release me.

As I sat on the hospital bed, one of the doctors who was taking his leave from my bedside to fetch the release forms, stated that he was amazed I was sitting up and talking, since people with my test results were normally in a catatonic state. Then, with tears welled up in his eyes, he stated that he was weeping at the thought that I, some-one whom he perceived as being so kind-hearted, was taking an early departure from this life.

His emotion was a more than pleasant surprise. I had just met him, and I didn't feel quite that adorable. However, I was delighted he felt such good vibrations coming from me. One of my aspirations in this lifetime is to be a truly good, kindhearted, saintly and beneficial pres-ence on the planet—a mystical performing arts muse, you could say. I wanted to be someone that could help transform the hearts and minds of souls, so they could live happily ever after in heavenly, honey like vibrations, within the heart of the eternal goodness from which all things manifest.

Anyways, let's get back to the reality of the situation. The doctor was still in a most distraught emotional state. He said that the world needed me to stay and that he was dismayed at my choice. He was convinced I would die within 24 hours without the needed surgery. I thanked him wholeheartedly, but insisted in a kind manner that I needed to leave the hospital.

When he left my room to get the papers, I started to hear the most amazing angelic music. I was completely enchanted by this celestial sound, and I thought to myself, *"This is the most divine music I have ever heard. It's amazing that this hospital is so hip, that they're playing such soul soothing heavenly music."*

Then, out of nowhere, the most brilliant holy light came flooding into the room from the wall just in front of me, and it started to ema-nate from the ceiling above, as well. First, I thought I was having an hallucination. Then, I thought for sure, *"I must be dying, I must be on the edge of life."*

I suddenly felt an infinite wave of pure, unconditional love washing over my entire being, a love so pure and so splendid, so vast, so limitless, and all embracing, that it took my breath away. I was immediately, and immensely, humbled at this wondrous sight. Then, I noticed that all my anxieties, even the fear of death and being crippled for life, were completely washed away, as was all of my pain. My mind was in a state of nirvana. I was beyond heavenly.

Next, a large luminescent angel appeared, radiating with a heavenly glow. He had a celestial compassionate persona, a pure sweet and Godly affection that was like nothing I'd ever seen or felt. I felt safe and secure, like I was resting in the arms of God's perfect compassionate immaculate mercy. I felt loved beyond my wildest dreams, being in the presence of this great and radiant holy being. I observed many other angels joining him, like a wonderful transcendental greeting party.

Then, the primary angel began to speak:

"We played the heavenly music so you would not be afraid when the bright light appeared before you. We wanted you to feel comforted, knowing you have the heart and soul of a divine devotional performing artist and are dedicated to the divine arts."

The most astonishing part was when the angel said, "We know you have been praying to God for many days now to give you permission to leave this world, and God lovingly wants you to know that you have his permission. You can now take leave of this life, and are more than welcome to join us, if you wish, in the golden-hearted land where you can sing and dance to your heart's content eternally for God."

Well as you could only imagine, my heart leapt with happiness. It was beyond my wildest dreams to have gotten an answer from God Himself, and to hear that I could come home to him right then and there! What greater audience would a devotional artist strive for than to perform for God himself and his entourage? The news was beyond my comprehension. I had received a glimpse of what it would be like to obtain the holiest of communion, and be favored in God's eyes. To put it mildly, I was taken aback that I, someone who had not accomplished any great spiritual feats or acts of global kindness, could have had this experience.

I was about to answer but couldn't speak, as the angels had rendered me speechless with their awesome angelic presence. However, in my heart, I was crying, begging, and pleading to say, *"Yes! Yes! I want to go with you. Please take me now! I want to dive into this immense kindness, to join you in the pure holy land of divine love, the compassionate sea of eternal bliss! As you angels are all the embodiment of divine tenderness, so mesmerizing and illuminating is your presence."*

And then in my mind I thought, *"My goodness, if these angels are of this magnitude, and bringing with them such a vast ocean of overwhelming goodness, then what must God be like?"*

Then, an illuminated realization entered into the core of my heart. As I felt the blissful glimmer of hope that, I too, someday could swim in the eternal river of benevolence with the Lord of all Lords. I knew at that point that this was where I wanted to be eternally. I had read once that the real goal of life is to use this life to navigate one's way back to the Divine of all. It is at this point that one never loses sight. I now knew that I needed to set my sights high, and stay the course, as this was the ultimate goal, the most highly prized treasure of all of existence. My heart was bursting with happiness at the mere thought of leaving this world with these amazing celestial beings. To drink from this fountain of divine ecstasy was already far beyond my wildest dream.

However, when I went to reply to them, in response to their invitation, I was unable to utter a word. I realized that I was in a state of such awe and reverence that I was rendered speechless. Then, after the silence between us, the head luminescent angel spoke these words, *"God would like you to stay here on earth, because you have more of his work to do in this world."*

I knew that God, through these luminescent beings, had answered my question, but I felt deeply despondent, yet elated at the same time. What a dilemma! What was I to say? Did I really have to give up my opportunity to enter into this amazing rapturous world? I wondered why I hadn't spoken up earlier when the angel originally made such an astonishing offer. He said I could leave this world!

In truth, though, I felt I hadn't been as effective in God's service as I wished I were. So I had to let go of the dream of letting my soul fly away freely with these immaculate angels to the land beyond paradise. At that moment, I understood that God's wish for me was to stay here. This was a test of my love for Him. At one of the darkest times of my life, here was the portal leading to an abyss of divine bliss. My body was almost sixty years old, and I had not made a significant impact in the world. Something I deeply hankered for was to be of some real use in His name.

I also thought about my own selfishness, having become puffed up for taking so long to accept what God had in store for me. Fortunately, the Lord and His angels are most forgiving and extraordinarily tolerant. I realized that my inability to speak up had been a sublunary part of the plan.

Though not completely committed to the outcome, I had to surrender my own dreams to fulfill God's request. With that stated, the angels lifted their hands toward me, and I could feel a blessing flowing from them into my soul. Then, sensing their coming departure, with a reverent heart, and hands offered in prayer, I gave them my humble veneration. Then, just as suddenly as this ocean of angelic radiance had appeared, they were gone. I felt an overwhelming feeling of elation, as I had just seen the faces of beings, who were most dear to the Lord of all.

A few minutes later, the doctor came back into the room with release papers, and to his surprise, I most happily signed them. My pain had completely subsided, and in its place, was a feeling of a soul replenished, revived and invigorated with supernatural purpose. As I walked out, my friend, who was waiting for me in the lobby, proclaimed, "Your face is glowing, you look like you just saw the face of God."

In turn I said, "You're right, I just saw his angels!" I proceeded to tell him the rest of the story. Needless to say, he was amazed.

Once I got home, I was baffled about how to take care of myself, or even what I could eat. Four days prior to my emergency room visit, I'd been having difficulty keeping anything down. This was partially caused by fear of the pain. When I digesting anything, including water, it would pelt out of my mouth like a wild projectile. I had also lost a great deal of weight. I was under seventy pounds, and was in a weaken state. Mustering up what strength I could, I again prayed to the angels, and I asked them to kindly guide me, as I was just coming back from the edge of the afterlife.

A few moments later, the angels materialized once again, but it was a different set of angels who were smaller in stature, and their vibration was very nurturing. To start, they indicated that they wanted to communicate via a form of telepathy, and it was through this means that they would guide me.

I began to feel like the chef in the movie Ratatouille, who was being trained by the little mouse, in the finer points of the culinary arts. This lighthearted interaction made me laugh, such a kindness and sweetness filled the air. These wonderful angels were my hero's. They allowed me to survive the perilous first night. The first step was to simply sip small amounts of water during the first twenty-four hours. Then, they guided me in creating a magical combination of fresh veggie juices and broths for the next two weeks. Little by little, they told me when to add various types of super-foods that were a little hardier in consistency, into my diet, but the food still needed to be blended for easy digestion. This wonderful guidance helped me obtain an unparalleled expedited healing. This was later confirmed by doctors.

For the next four months, these kindhearted angels visited daily, and guided me, in order to replenish and revitalize my body. Just being around them gave such tremendous spiritual inspiration! It is worth noting that they made sure I avoided fried foods and oils. They were emphatic about avoiding processed foods and junk foods, including seemingly harmless items such as potato chips. Even wheat, tofu, and dairy were to be avoided. Being a big potato chip fan, it was a real sacrifice, but worth it. They were especially explicit about the elimination of refined sugars, honey and agave. Being a good student, I eliminated all processed foods from my diet.

They had given me more than just the formula for a healthy vegetarian diet. They had given me a miraculous super-food diet, with the right amounts, and at the right time. I am convinced that this diet is good for anyone who needs to heal his or her body, or get to a balanced body weight. If you visit our website, you'll find many helpful tips on how to follow this angelic miracle diet. It also will help you obtain the ideal weight and maintain it. It is very lean, so you can eat as much as you like.

The angels also directed me to get acupuncture, and suggested daily yoga, or Tai chi. They also introduced the most fluid, beautiful, healing, meditative, devotional dance. You can find some of the movements on the web site. Best of all, they gifted my voice with a wonderful healing tone. I found that when I combined the vocals with the movements they taught me, a prayerful, spontaneous interpretation would emerge. Later, when I was so very blessed to be able to render this devotional performance, their blessings helped me to inspire audiences to connect with their own wonderful intuitive gifts, filling their souls with the light of angelic love. I felt a greater connection with my life purpose, my dream, to be a musical muse of enlightenment. One day, I hoped to capture the essence of this angelic, celestial emergence, this portal of time that I had experienced with these most incredible beings. I wanted to somehow relay this in a creative flow in movement and in sound.

Intuitively, I feel that all artists, be it performance or otherwise, are here to become muses of enlightenment. Our higher calling is to maintain this positive, uplifting channel, which allows us to funnel this creative resonance coming from the spiritual realms. Letting the divine goodness flow through your soul in pure intention can allow a sweet Godly essence to unfold. I find it is all about stepping out of the way, and letting the higher beings use you, as a holy vessel, for the creative devotional arts. Because of this experience, I believe that there are other angelic dimensions that exist simultaneously alongside this realm, which beckon and encourage us into the more mystical, magical aspects of life.

During this time of healing, people commented that the quality of my speaking voice had changed. They stated that they felt healed simply from having a conversation with me, even on the phone, and when they hung up, they felt deeply inspired and uplifted. I realized how easy it is to forget that inspiration is coming from the Divinity of all. At times, the ego wants to step in and claim ownership of something that belongs to the domain of the higher absolute. Fortunately, the Infinite simply would not allow such vibrations to enter, and most kindly make the needed corrections. So, the discovery for me, was that the flow of grace was dependent on being in this selfless, devotional mindset, similar to the mood of helping someone in need.

These kinds of miraculous experiences encourage us to fill our hearts, minds, and souls with good thoughts, actions, and deeds. They inspire us to be kinder, more positive, embrace greater cheerfulness, deeper compassionate, and be spontaneously helpful. So, give credit where it is due—to higher angelic beings and to God Himself. I now see myself as His grateful instrument, put on this earth to reflect His Divine works, and to inspire the people of the world in whatever expression of His they feel most drawn to.

I have come to understand that the gift of being pure of heart allows unconditional love and mercy to flow through. I always say I am the Lords masterpiece in progress, yet to reach the fullest expression.

It helps to tune in with a humble heart, to wait patiently for the blessings to arrive, as this gives deeper entrance into the place of anointed intentions. When this wave of creative bliss flows, the dance from the higher planes of existence will be easy, and at times the Godly avatars themselves may become manifest.

During the four months that I spent with these amazing angelic beings, there were other Godly deva's from a higher level of the Divine spectrum that manifested. These encounters are revealed in greater detail in my book, *Angels and Avatars*.

My recovery became such an amazing journey, that whenever the opportunity arises, I do my best to recreate these incredible, inspiring, transcendental experiences within my performances and talks, whenever possible. Doing so has become the center point of my life's purpose. To gift others with a glimpse into this exquisite holy realm, so they too, even for a moment, feel the ocean of this pure sweet love that God has for us, a love beyond imagination, would be a dream come true. Join us, and enjoy viewing some of these devotional performances on our website: www.TheQuantumVocalist.com.

I hope that my gift to you will make your day a little brighter, a little sweeter, a little kinder, and more enlivened spiritually. We all need each other to help uplift us from time to time.

Another brilliant gem of wisdom from the angels was the guidance to create a self-help hypnosis recording combined with NLP. So, I found a good practitioner and later became certified in both modalities. We now offer these wonderful mind tools as an added service on our web site, for those who wish to feel their wonderful effects.

In combination, I have incorporated cutting-edge sonic healing sounds and music that supports deep subconscious change and accelerates learning. These methods allowed me to fully integrate healthy eating habits and lifestyle choice. I was compelled to absorb myself in them, since they were a major component in maintaining a healthier lifestyle regimen.

As I became more proficient at implementing this wonderful healing program, I realized it would be helpful to millions of others who spend thousands of dollars annually on products, programs, potions, and pills to cure themselves or fix bad habits, such as eating too much, eating unhealthy foods, or not getting enough exercise. Many people find it difficult to stick with their goals and good intentions to be healthy, happy, wise and successful, in all areas of their lives. I believe if they could find real health, success, and happiness, in these areas, through the use of the best personal mind-training programs, it would be a great blessing. Millions of lives could be transformed. I became certified in these modalities, specifically to be of greater service in the healing of people's bodies, minds, and souls. I firmly believe that whoever conquers their mind conquers their world.

It is my hope and prayer that people will spread this news far and wide so that everyone who needs this kind of help can have access to it. Also, the cost of the products is done as a suggested donation, which makes it affordable for everyone. Most of all, we want the freedom to not be ruled by the mind and the senses. We want to be bold and embrace self-love, while we take a stand for our own wellbeing and happiness. Remember that our voices hold the power key to global harmony.

Being the poster child for transformation through my illness and subsequent recovery, I came to understand that we are meant to be a gift in this world, creating and leaving behind a divine legacy. Find what makes your heart sing and embrace that higher calling, even if it's simply volunteering for a charity on weekends. All forms of devotion given freely from the heart are never lost, and are always rewarded. This is the winning formula to finding the gems within, and gaining access to unconditional love. This free ticket will support your journey back to health and harmony, and ultimately, back to God.

A prayer of thanks, each and every day, is now my daily path. I will always feel eternally indebted to the Lord and His miraculous avatars and angels. When I ponder the immaculate vast love that the Lord has for us, I wonder if it is possible to repay such a remarkable gift—a gift that defies explanation. Even if it was the best and finest of all things this world has to offer, would ever be enough?

I know in my heart of hearts that all God wants is our sincere love, a pure love, a faithful love, a trusting love, an unconditional love being the crest jewel of such communion. An untainted love is the most precious gift we can give. In return, it gives freedom from all the daily cares of this world. When you see this world for what it truly is, a place of learning about who we are and why we're here, then we understand that a heart filled with love, devotion, and enthusiasm, is the best thing for ourselves and for others.

It took me many months to regain my voice and my health. I began to live a much more spiritually driven life, and two years later, I went back to the doctor and was declared lupus-free. Three years later, I married the love of my life, the man of my dreams, an amazingly wonderful human being, who is deeply committed to his spiritual path and brilliant music ministry. He has journeyed on this glorious path for more than forty years. He is a man who embodies "The Genius of Devotion." As a devotional couple, with God at the center of our lives, we are blessed to create magical, spiritual productions that are uplifting and inspiring.

Through this beloved marital union and partnership, I have been able to share my voice of devotion, and my divine dance, at a much higher level of spiritual expression. When the angels said that I had more spiritual work to do on the planet, I could not have guessed it would be so enjoyable. I now understand the phrase, "If we take one step to God, He takes a million steps to us." He gives us the unparalleled richness of life, and a vibrant inner world.

If you are interested in knowing more about the angelic diet, the healing lifestyle, the recipes and the music that the angels shared with me, the book and video are available on my web site, www.TheQuantumVocalist.com, where you can also learn about, and experience, our current and upcoming devotional musical performances.

Health and Longevity: Benefits of Singing

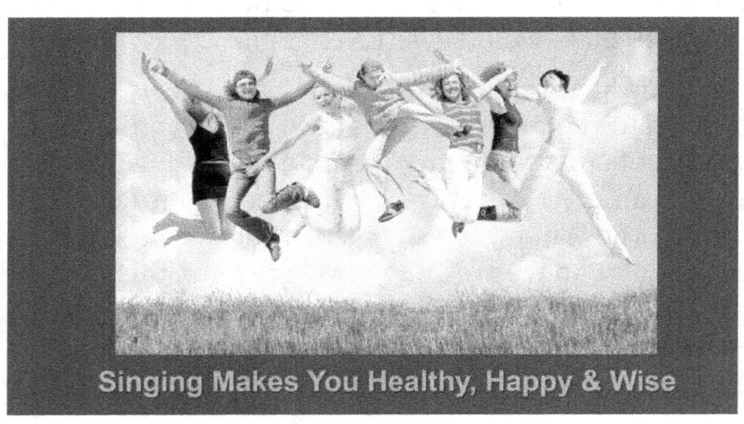

Singing releases endorphins in the brain, providing a natural high, and keeping the brain in peak condition. Research from the University of Kansas Medical Center states that people with the most musical training had the best mental acuity, and scored the highest on brain functioning tests, regardless of their ages.

Anyone who sings, or chants, knows that a daily practice heightens spatial awareness and intelligence. Additional benefits include improved concentration and increased speech abilities. Those who received regular singing instruction have shown a marked advancement in reading and language skills. It has been confirmed that students who sing enjoy a startling increase in SAT scores.

The benefits of singing, however, can go further than raising test scores and levels of health and well-being. Singing greatly enhances the quality of your life. By implementing regular singing lessons into you and your child's life, you can:

- Stimulate brain growth
- Positively affect emotional perceptions and attitudes
- Reduce emotional and physical stress
- Enhance motor skill development
- Improve language ability, including vocabulary
- Enhance social abilities
- Improve reading, writing, and mathematical skills
- Improve overall academic skills
- Improve memory skills
- Increase and improve recall functions
- Enhance the ability to solve problems
- Provide the tools to find lasting inner happiness, peace, and purpose

I cannot stress enough the benefits that can be achieved when the music is spiritual, inspiring and positive in nature. Singing, a modality available to all of us, can have a potent and wonderful effect on the body, mind, and soul. I personally guarantee that you will find so much happiness from singing, and uttering the holy names of God, that you will become hooked on the high of this particular form of singing. It can help control blood pressure and stabilize your emotions, even in the most challenging of situations. It can help you become a better communicator and develop healthier self-esteem. From a material point of view, the development of your singing talents often makes others view you as a more valuable, and beneficial person, to your family and community.

This perception provides the vocalist with the gift of greater popularity, enviable reputation, influence, and fame, which leads to an upgrade in life, bringing in meaningful opportunities. When this is dovetailed with spiritual life mastery skills, you can live a more vibrant life and cultivate a greater sphere of influence in the world. Even if you don't embrace transcendental singing as your vocation, just add it to your life whenever you can.

Uplifting songs are the salve of comfort during any crisis in life. When you sing your heart out to God, He will hear your cries, and you will feel His immaculate loving kindness magically appear within your life. Just have faith, stay the course, and one day, His Divine love will find its way into your life. Just be patient. Love takes time. If you aspire to this level of faith, then repeat:

No matter what it takes, I will never give up.

It's never too late to feel spiritually great.

There are endless ways that singing devotional songs make our hearts and spirits feel better. Clients, who hum or sing along with their favorite devotional music or work with a vocal therapist along these same lines, experience a reduction in anxiety, depression, irritability, frustration, anger, and hopelessness. When they get sick, singing helps them heal much faster.

People with cancer have found that listening, singing, or humming along to their favorite devotional songs, decreases pain, fear, and anxiety. They experience better blood pressure levels and an improvement in their mood. Singing inspiring songs conjures up encouraging, reassuring, positive emotions when you need them the most, because it provides your brain with a calming, healing, euphoric effect.

Parents who give their children singing lessons are doing their child's brains a big favor. Positive inspiring singing is linked to better academic test results and overall educational performance.

In 2008, the journal *Brain* published research that found singing, or listening, to inspiring music was linked with improved memory and attention among stroke patients when compared with patients not singing, or listening, to anything. Researchers from the Group Health Research Institute reported that patients who received ten one-hour massages had the same decreased anxiety symptoms three months later as people who simply sang, or hummed, while listening to soothing spiritual music.

Obviously, singing has greater health advantages than most of us realize. If you're not convinced yet, the next time you feel worried, anxious, or sick, take some time to sing, hum, or listen to uplifting music. I guarantee your mood, and your symptoms, will improve.

Always take good care of your voice and it will take care of you in the most amazing and wonderful ways. Below is an excerpt from an address given by Karl Paulnack, a music instructor at the Boston Conservatory:

> *"The human spirit is an unquenchable expression of who we are. Singing is one of the ways in which we say, 'I am alive and my life has meaning.'"*

On the evening of September 11, 2001, singing was the first organized activity in New York. People sang around fire stations. They sang "We Shall Overcome." Many people sang "America, the Beautiful." The first organized public event was Brahms' Requiem, at Lincoln Center, with the New York Philharmonic. Our first communal response to that historic event was a concert. That was the beginning of a sense that life might go on. The U. S. Military secured the airspace. Yet, that night, singing, the arts, and music were the heart of the program.

Singing and music are not just parts of "arts and entertainment", as the newspapers would have us believe. They are not a luxury, a lavish thing that we fund from leftovers of our budgets. They are not a plaything, an amusement, or a pastime. Singing and music are basic needs of human survival. Singing and music are the way we make sense of our lives, the way we express feelings when we have no words, a way for us to understand things with our hearts when we can't make sense of them with our minds.

Some of you may know Samuel Barber's heart-wrenchingly beautiful piece, "Adagio For Strings." It was the background music for the Oliver Stone movie, *Platoon*, a film about the Vietnam War. That piece of music has the ability to crack your heart open like a walnut. It can make you feel sadness you didn't know you had. Music can slip beneath our conscious reality, and tap into what's going on inside us, in the same way a good therapist does.

Very few of us have ever been to a wedding where there was no music. There might have been a little music. There might have been some really bad music. However, with few exceptions, there is some music. In addition, something very predictable happens at weddings; namely, people get emotional. Usually, there is some musical moment where the action of the wedding stops, and someone sings or plays the flute. Even if the music is lame, even if the quality isn't good, thirty or forty percent of the people who cry at weddings do so a couple of moments after the music starts.

Music allows us to move around pieces of ourselves and rearrange our insides so we can express what we feel, even when we can't talk about it. Can you imagine watching Avatar, *Brother Sun Sister Moon,* or *the Matrix* with dialogue, but no music? What is it about the music swelling up at just the right moment in ET that makes all the softies in the audience start crying at exactly the same moment? I guarantee if you showed the movie with the music stripped out, it wouldn't happen that way. Music expresses the relationship between invisible internal objects.

I have played a little less than a thousand concerts so far, in places that I thought were important. I liked playing in Carnegie Hall in New York. I enjoyed playing in Paris. It made me happy to please the critics in St. Petersburg, Russia. I have played for people I thought were important, such as music critics of major newspapers and foreign heads of state. However, the most important concert of my entire life took place in a nursing home, in a small mid-western town, a few years ago.

I was playing with a very dear friend of mine who is a violinist. We began, as we often do, with Aaron Copland's "Sonata," which was written during World War II, and dedicated to a friend of Copland's, a young pilot who was shot down during the war. We often talk to our audience about the pieces we are going to play rather than providing them with written program notes. In this case, since we began the concert with this piece, we decided to come out and play the music without explanation. We could talk about it later in the program.

Midway through the piece, an elderly man seated in a wheelchair near the front of the concert hall began to weep. This man, whom I met later, had been a soldier. Now in his seventies, it was clear from his buzz cut hair, square jaw, and general demeanor that he had spent a good deal of his life in the military. I thought it a little odd that someone would be moved to tears by that particular movement, but it wasn't the first time I'd heard crying in a concert. We went on and finished the piece.

When we came out to play the next piece on the program, we decided to talk about both the first and second pieces. We described the circumstances in which the Copland piece was written and mentioned its dedication to a downed pilot. The man in the audience became so disturbed that he left the auditorium. I figured we wouldn't see him again, but he came backstage afterwards to explain himself.

"During World War II," he said, "I was a pilot. I was in an aerial combat situation where one of my team's planes was hit. I watched my friend bail out. I watched his parachute open, but the Japanese planes returned, and machine-gunned across the parachute cords to separate the parachute from the pilot. I watched my friend drop away into the ocean. He was lost. I haven't thought about this for many years, but during that first piece of music you played, the memory returned to me so vividly, I relived it. I didn't understand why it was happening right then, but when you came out to explain that his piece of music was written to commemorate a lost pilot, it was a little more than I could handle. How does music do that? How did it touch those feelings and memories in me?"

The Greeks say that music is the study of invisible relationships between internal objects. That concert in the nursing home was the most important work I have ever done. To play for this veteran and help him connect with Aaron Copland, to connect them with memories of their lost friends, to help him remember his friend, that is my work. This is why music matters.

I want assure you that you're not here necessarily to become an entertainer. You don't have to see yourself. You don't have to have anything to sell. Being a musician isn't about dispensing a product. I don't see myself as an entertainer. I'm a lot closer to a paramedic, a firefighter, or a rescue worker. I'm here to become a therapist for the human soul, a spiritual version of a chiropractor, or a physical therapist, someone who works to achieve harmony, health, and happiness.

I encourage you not only to master music, but to save the planet. If there is a future wave of wellness on this planet that brings harmony, peace, an end to war, mutual understanding, equality, and fairness, I don't expect it will come from a government, a military force, or a corporation. I don't expect it will come from the religions of the world, which seem to bring us as much war as they do peace. If there is a future of peace for humankind, if there is to be understanding of how these invisible, internal things fit together, I expect it will come from artists, because that's what we do.

The Love of Singing: The Legacy Passed On

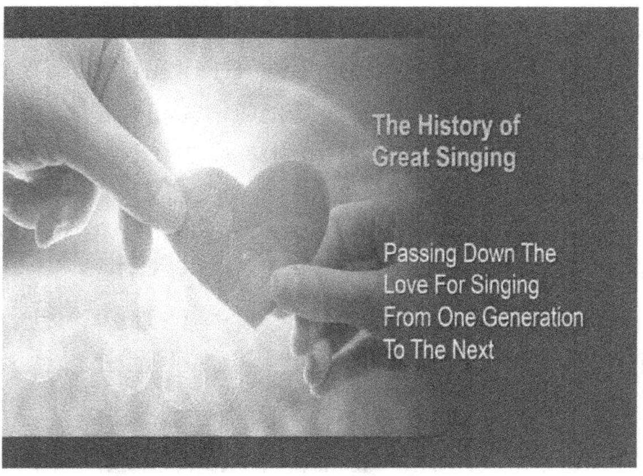

One of the greatest gifts we can give our children is the love of singing. This wonderful art form not only brings hours and hours of inner happiness, it gives children the tools they need to deal with the ups-and-downs of life, making the benefits immeasurable. When I was growing up, my mother encouraged me to sing. I didn't realize what a gift she was giving me. When she left this world, it finally dawned on me what an immense service she had done in protecting and preserving my life on all levels.

To this day, I sing her praises for this amazing blessing, as your children will when you encourage them, and nurture this art in their souls. This cherished art form is one that has been passed down from one generation to the next, an oral tradition that can bond the past, present, and future through singing.

A World of Expression

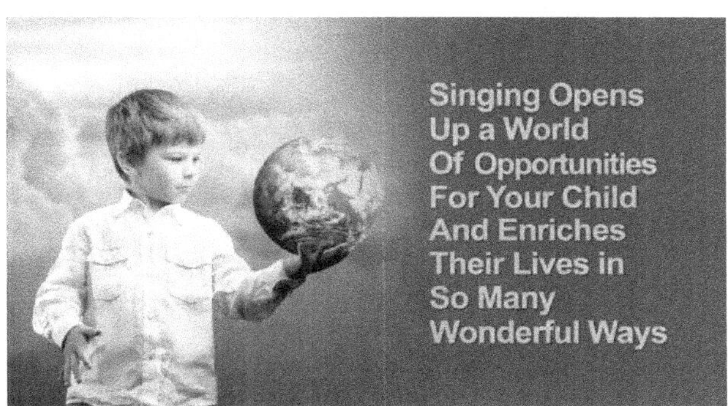

For children, singing positive, or spiritual, music opens up a world of expression, creativity, and empowerment. Singing leads to higher self-esteem and provides children with a sense of direction. This leads to the attainment of better social standing, and gaining positive communication skills and interactions. Parents, guardians, family members, or benefactors who give this precious gift of singing to a child provide him or her with a place of inner sanctuary, shelter, strength, and a positive creative outlet.

A Gift That Lasts a Lifetime

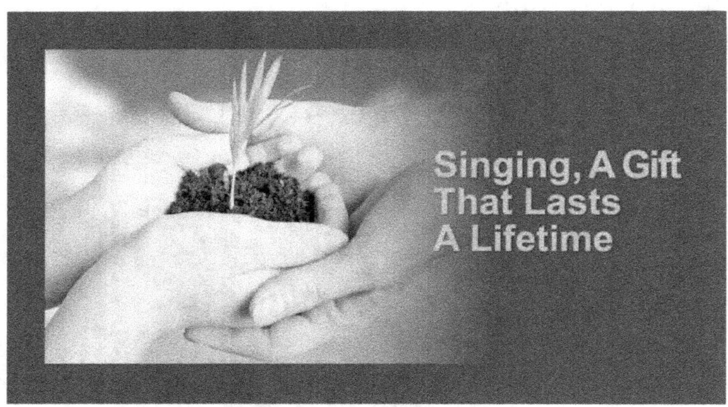

Children who learn how to sing at an early age go on to become better problem solvers and achieve higher academic scores. Singing provides so many wonderful gains for children when the seeds of singing are planted an early age. With proper guidance and nurturing, their creative thirst, inspiration and love for the art will blossom and flourish.

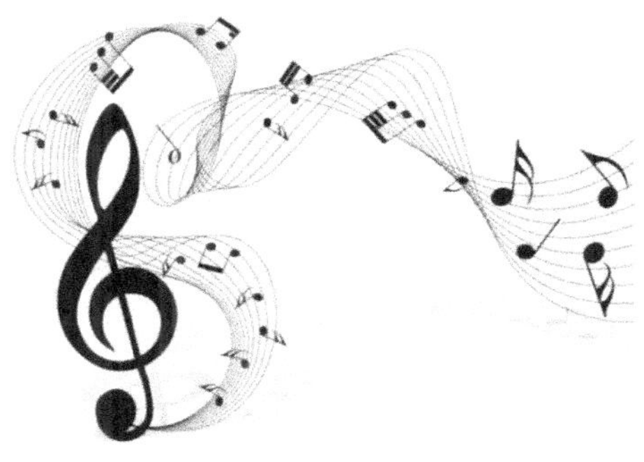

CHAPTER TEN

A Higher Calling

A Singer's Life Purpose for Living: Celebrating Life!

Sound vibration is one of the most powerful forces in the universe. Combined with divine names, as in gospel music, spiritual hymns, sacred mantras, or devotional chanting, these vibrations transcend space and time and bring you closer to God.

When you sing holy names, they are infused with transcendental qualities, and holy beings can actually be present with you. If you sing mundane material, the words don't have the ability to uplift anyone, or be present.

Quantum Physics come into play when you utter transcendental sounds, since they deal with frequencies of the highest and purest types. These holy names, words, and sounds carry a supreme vibratory potency on a transcendental level. In this vein, using your voice to glorify the Divine, no matter your spiritual belief system, is the greatest gift you can give to humankind. It is a celebration of the soul, and the highest use of a singer's life. When you sing in the highest vibrations, you become a muse of enlightenment, and of God's grace. This weaves a magical spell that will awaken the heart of your listeners. The gift is otherworldly, which brings happiness, a kind of happiness their soul is seeking.

Sing Your Prayers, Dance Your Dreams

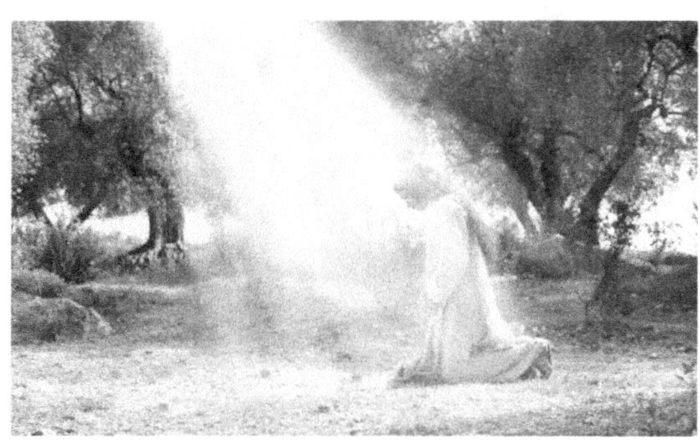

It doesn't matter what you call God: Lord Jesus, Buddha, The Universe, Sri Krishna, Spirit, Sri Rama, or Allah. He has millions of names, and they appear in this world with a particular spiritual flavor. This supreme design is for the soul who finds that divine expression consistent with his or her natural inclinations.

Seeing the Divine is the solution to every problem on the planet. If people took up singing, or chanting, of spiritual, inspiring, devotional music, and began dancing to sacred sounds, they would become so high, and feel so much love in their hearts that they would never need to take external stimulants or drugs. They would forgive all, and never harm anyone, because their soul would be overflowing with God's unconditional compassion. The Supreme One has given us many paths to find our way home, according to our likes and dislikes.

Here is a fun analogy: Some people like vanilla ice cream, while others like strawberry. The expression of God has many forms, such as Jesus, Krishna, Buddha, Shiva, Allah, Jehovah, Vishnu, and so forth. His love is so vast that He gave us these many forms in order for the living being to choose which expression of divinity they acclimate most with. With this simple, yet profound, concept realized within this world, there would be no separation, no conflicts, and no wars. Instead, a mutual respect for other's beliefs would emerge, blossom, and thrive. Here is another great revelation: If you closely examine religious traditions, you'll find a powerful thread of commonality running through them all, such as being a good human, developing kindness, and showing compassion for others. On an esoteric platform, it makes sense, as all religions are coming from the same source, namely, God. Hence, the basic structure that draws the parallel, the connective fiber in these traditions, embraces the soul to develop and maintain a moral compass.

With this in mind, one could eliminate discrimination towards others' beliefs. One could view the world as a global community, where everyone is part of the family of man. Under such a view, natural harmony and understanding would prevail. The understanding that we are all beloved children of God would give way to a greater sense of peace, and harmony would naturally emerge. We would seek to understand each other's hearts, souls, and minds. We would want to find the common ground, in order to care for and serve one another, viewing everyone as a spirit soul to be respected, protected and cared for.

An inner connectedness between souls, and the connection to a higher consciousness is one of the keys that can transform our global community.

Everyone needs to cultivate acts of forgiveness, tolerance, forbearance, and compassion. In Hawaii, we call this Ho'oponopono, as acts of forgiveness that will bring about inner strength, power, empathy, and a higher purpose in life.

The handbook for a good life encourages us to become compassionate human beings, who chooses to be a beneficial presence on the planet. This takes the form of "Blissipline," a term that a friend, Rev. Michael Beckwith, coined. Blissipline is a state of inner contentment, a stepping-stone to enlightenment, found in directing your mind, speech, action and senses. In the process, you will find greater contentment, fulfillment, peace, and ecstasy.

Whatever you wrap your mind around is what you will emulate in life. I believe that singing spiritually inspired music is the perfect solutions to our social problems. Such vocal engagement helps the consciousness fly high. So, enjoy life to the highest degree possible. "Sing your prayers and dance your divine dreams."

You might find yourself being happy for good reason.

The Formula to Balance and Bliss:
Discovering and Developing the Voice of the Soul

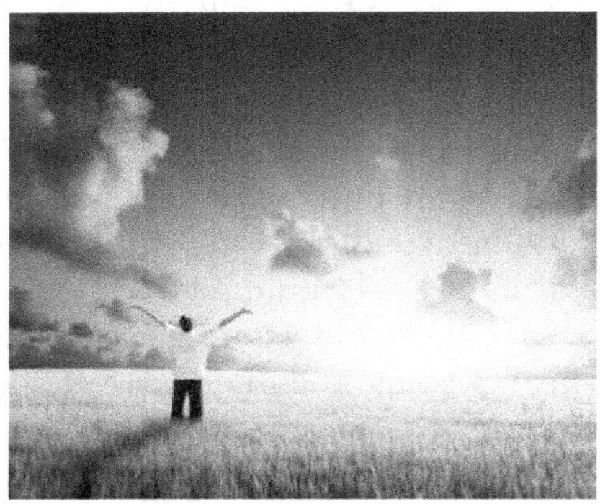

Finding your life's purpose is the key to bringing greater bliss and balance in life. Singing anointed music makes you whole. It makes you feel valuable. It makes your life worthwhile. This daily lyrical meditation, coming from your soul, offers you solace in your communion with the Creator. I'm talking about lasting emotional freedom from the world as you attain inner peace, paradise, and harmony. It brings inner spiritual meaning, as well as material longevity.

I believe that singers have a higher calling, a divine purpose to be spiritual muses, to bring in uplifting, beautiful, supernatural experiences to the world around us, through songs that give voice to the soul. Join us and become part of the global solution. Take your place, among millions of souls, dedicated to becoming global change agents. Raise your voice and be one of the souls leading this harmonic change. Together, we can stand as beacons of hope in a world that needs transcendental vibrations.

My beloved husband shares these insights with me, which profoundly describe the various levels of singing. He is connected to the moods and intentions they hold. This is his description of sacred singing:

"We are all instrumental and not the doers. The absolute Divine of all is acting through us to give us guidance and inspirations. The voice needs to not be generated by the throat any more, but to naturally spring up from the bottom of one's heart. Sound vibrations are carried away by ether, prana, the subtle energy that penetrates all elements of matter and spirit, and are imbued with our deepest and hidden intentions. Sound vibrations don't lie. Like spiritual fingerprints, they are the reflections of our inner truth. Our voice reflects our ideals, or the mood in which we are, when we sing."

The universal law of resonance effect describes reciprocation with the receptor-listener.

- When the vibes of the voice come from the throat, they touch the throat of the listener, as in someone who has a trained voice.
- When the voice comes from the guts, it touches the guts, as in rock music
- When the sound comes from the intellect, it touches the intellect of the listener, as in jazz.
- When the sound comes from the higher mind, it resonates with the higher mind of the listeners, as in classical music and opera.
- When the voice is socially emotional, it resonates with the social emotions of the listeners, as in popular songs on the radio.
- Finally, when the waves of sound come from the soul, they touch the souls of the listeners.

This is what we want. We want to vibrate in the heart of the listeners. We want a resonance from a spark of God to a spark of God. We want this sweet direct connection.

Voices of Ahimsa—Spreading Hope, Purpose and Saving Lives: Gift of Singing Worldwide

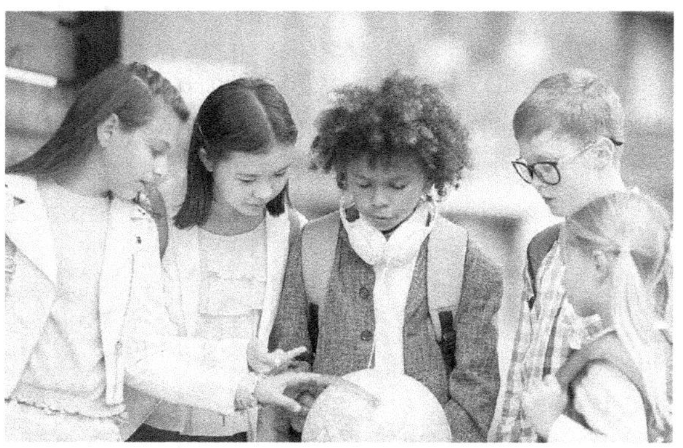

Singing is a cherished art form that is passed down from one generation to the next. It is a tradition that bonds the past, present, and future through song.

You can help! "Voices Of Ahimsa" is seeking to raise the funds needed to give millions of children around the world the gift of singing, a gift that will last a lifetime. "Voices Of Ahimsa" is a 501 (c) 3 non-profit organization.

The Mission:

> To inspire, bring purpose, give direction, give the gift of accelerated learning skills—and save lives—through the gift of music and free singing lesson to millions of at-risk, underprivileged children, or those living in warring regions around the world.

Much of the violence in schools, at home, in the streets, and in places of worship, can be linked to types of music and media. If parents, and society at large, make the neurological connection between what they and their children are hearing and seeing, they would realize that these things contribute to a person's consciousness, and how he or she interacts with the world.

Singing and playing positive, inspired, and devotional music, gives children a creative outlet, and empowers them with a sense of purpose and self-worth. Singing enhances and accelerates their learning skills, and helps them become more innovative and inspired. It brings them personal satisfaction, and is a viable alternative to drugs, violence, and hopelessness.

Learning to sing and play music is a life-enriching experience that gives children the promise of a brighter future, and makes them more valued members of their families, communities, and society as a whole. Singing creates a supportive environment for children to grow into adulthood, and in the process, to develop a healthier self-respect and self-assurance.

A good example of the power of music: Recently, one of my friends lost a family member to suicide. It was heart breaking for their family to experience such a loss. They were able to trace the connection between the music the person was listening to and the action that followed. This person wrote on his body that suicide was the only solution. It made me think, "If a person does not get the higher information that resonates with their intellect, they'll feel that suicide is the only way out."

Surely if the general populous knew the power that music has on the mind, they could then help their children make better choices. Holy scriptures reveal that if someone throws away the gift of the life that God gives them, they will have the opportunity to atone through a ghost body, and remain in that body, until their natural time arrives to depart this world. Apparently, a ghost state of being is a hundred times worse than the suffering of the earthly body, when they took their life. It seems that they will remain in that condition until their natural time comes. Therefore, a great motivating factor is to share with others this ever-important information, so they know that taking their life is not a solution. Communion through prayer with divinity is the solution.

Our life is meant for the most wonderful spiritual experiences. The way to journey into these magical places is through the power of prayer, whether in song, spoken word, or chant.

In order to help bring about such positive change in the world, we advocate and support sites like: www.VoicesofAhimsa.org.

A portion of all proceeds from the sale of this book go to help support this organization, which offers a solution to these growing problems. The vision is to gift children and youth around the world with inspired singing. VOA gives hope to youngsters who are at risk, living in poor economic conditions, or warring regions. VOA helps to usher in a brighter future for these children, and in the process, it saves lives.

The Goal of "Voices Of Ahimsa" is to bring together children from around the world to participate in virtual and live choirs, where they sing songs of hope, peace, and goodwill.

VOA is seeking to raise the funds needed to give millions of children around the world the gift of singing, a gift that will last a lifetime. You can help make the world a better place; simply visit www.VoicesOfAhimsa.org, and donate or volunteer today.

Singing Transforms the World
Be a Part of the Global Shift

In parting, friends, I wish you all the best in your inspired vocal journey. May it bring you a lifetime of bliss, comfort, and inner harmony. May your voice be a source of happiness and solace to all who have the good fortune of hearing you. May you find your path illuminated through this most amazing art.

As a singer, you embody the power of owning such a miraculous vocal instrument that brings about incredible shifts in the environment around you.

Therefore, my wish for you is that you become, ever more, a remarkable presence on the planet, an agent of positive change, and ultimately, that you embrace your soul's purpose along the way.

As vocalists, we take our listeners on a magical, musical journey, providing them with the positive insights and support needed to illuminate their path, giving greater purpose to life. The gift of song is one of the highest acts of compassion we can give to others, and one of the greatest gifts we can give to ourselves.

As singers, we are creative narrators, and our vocal story connects us to the world around us, bringing faith, hope, and the promise of a brighter day. Our songs can open up hearts, inspire minds, and enliven souls. The magic of singing can take the most tragic moments and create a poetic, lyrical masterpiece that gives solace, and speeds up emotional and physical healing.

For many of us, the transcendental arts are our most treasured sacred service. We offer this to our friends, families, and global community, and most of all, to God. It is one of the greatest acts of unconditional kindness that we can give. This spontaneous inspiration to create springs forth from an endless well of spiritual love that will never run dry.

The positive results are innumerable! The choice to change from sadness to a state of happiness can be instantaneous. Changing your mood can happen in the blink of an eye, bringing tranquility to your heart and that of others. Through the magic of your voice you can give this amazing blessing to yourself and to the world, and in God's eyes, you will be highly prized.

On this journey called life, you can choose to enjoy the amazing inner happiness that comes for being on a path that's filled with spiritual purpose. And be the wonderful instrument of divine hope, compassion and wisdom that your meant to be. A muse of God's divine light, faith & unconditional love. As this makes life worth living, and surly a life well lived.

GLOSSARY

Embouchure:

This refers to the way in which a singer applies, or shapes, the mouth to create the perfect resonant sound.

Register:

A range of tones in the human voice produced by a particular vibratory pattern of the vocal folds. These registers include modal voice (or normal voice), vocal fry, falsetto, and the whistle register. Registers originate in laryngeal function.

Vocal Range:

The measure of the breadth of pitches that a human voice can phonate. Although the study of vocal range has little practical application in terms of speech, it is a topic of study within linguistics, phonetics, speech, and language pathology, in relation to the study of tonal languages and certain types of vocal disorders.

The most common application of the term "vocal range" is in the context of singing, where it is used as one of the defining characteristics for classifying singing voices into groups known as voice types.

Splatting:

A common phenomenon, "Splatting the vowel," is pulling up a bit of chest, or a lack of perfect cord closure. Bring awareness to this as you do exercises and narrow your vowels. The shape of your mouth affects the tone of the vowel. The wider your mouth, the wider the vowel and the more you will splat the sound.

Three and Four Voices:

1. Make Voices: Countertenor, Tenor, Baritone, and Bass

2. Female Voices: Soprano, Mezzo Soprano, Contralto

Vocal Mapping:

Navigating with vocal ease through the Voices

Voice Box:

The larynx, commonly called the voice box, is an organ in the neck of amphibians, reptiles, and mammals involved in breathing, sound production, and protecting the trachea against food aspiration. It manipulates pitch and volume. The larynx houses the vocal folds (vocal chords), which are essential for phonation. The vocal folds are situated just below the area where the tract of the pharynx splits into the trachea and the esophagus. Source: Wikipedia, the free encyclopedia